CORSICA AND SARDINIA

A Visitor's Guide

Gerry Crawshaw

W.H. ALLEN · LONDON
1987

Set in Times New Roman by
Phoenix Photosetting, Chatham
Printed and bound in Great Britain by
Mackays of Chatham Ltd, Kent
for the Publishers, W.H. Allen & Co. Plc
44 Hill Street, London W1X 8LB

ISBN 0 491 03147 5

DEDICATION

To my goddaughter, Maria

CORSICA
AND SARDINIA
A Visitor's Guide

Also by Gerry Crawshaw and published by W.H. Allen

TURKEY THE BEAUTIFUL
PORTUGAL – A VISITOR'S GUIDE

CONTENTS

CORSICA AND SARDINIA –
AN INTRODUCTION

'There is no denying that most of use, when we arrive at a place,
immediately think of others places to which we may go from it.'
ROBERT LYND

CORSICA AND SARDINIA. . . . two beautiful holiday islands
practically touching one another in the Mediterranean, both
having a great deal in common as far as spectacular scenery,
wonderful beaches and attractive holiday resorts are concerned,
but each with its own particular appeal, charm and attractions.

This book is intended as a practical guide to both islands for use
before a visit, in helping to choose where to go, how to get there,
and what to see; and also as a useful reference for when you are
there, with pen-portraits of the principal resorts, towns and villages
on both islands, lists of hotels, holiday villages and restaurants that
enjoy good reputations, other useful addresses and telephone
numbers, and places of interest in and near the resorts and towns.

Making a choice between Corsica or Sardinia is practically
impossible, since they both have so much to offer the
holidaymaker; but, fortunately, there are excellent ferry links
between the two islands, with frequent services in the summer
months, so that you need not restrict yourself to one island, but can
sample them both if you wish during the same holiday.

Less than 12 km separate Corsica and Sardinia, bordered on the
west by the Mediterranean and on the east by the Tyrrhenian Sea.
Corsica, with a total land area of 8,722 square km, roughly
comparable with the area of Wales, is much smaller than Sardinia
(24,089 square km) but is greater in area than the largest of the
Balearic islands, and much larger than all the remaining islands of
the western Mediterranean.

Although politically part of France, Corsica is much closer
geographically to Italy. Not only is it a short boat ride from
Sardinia, but the city of Bastia is only 82 km from the Italian

mainland, whereas the nearest point of mainland France is 160 km distant. Thus, while being a French island, Corsica bears a very strong Italian influence, not least in its cuisine, with pizzerias, as opposed to brasseries, having sprung up in practically every town, resort and village.

Corsica is arguably the more beautiful of the two islands, variously described as the 'mountain in the sea,' 'isle of beauty', and 'scented isle'. It boasts superb mountain scenery, again arguably more beautiful and dramatic than that of its neighbour, and an excellent choice of really delightful holiday resorts, many developed from picturesque fishing ports and occupying superb coastal sites complete with ancient citadels, watchtowers and ancient churches.

Being smaller than Sardinia, Corsica is also easier to get round by car, making it a good choice for those who prefer the freedom of touring holidays, though most of the roads are extremely narrow and follow tortuous courses through the mountain ranges, so you need strong nerves and a good head for heights. Corsica, indeed, is much more mountainous than its neighbour; in fact, it is the most mountainous island in the Mediterranean, only Mount Etna, in Sicily (3,200 metres), exceeding Corsica's highest peak, Monte Cinto (2,710 metres); while no other island has such an unbroken mass of mountainous terrain unrelieved by extensive lowlands.

Corsica probably does not rate as highly as Sardinia as far as public transport is concerned, and what does exist tends to be slow and infrequent. Even the train services are none too quick, so hiring a car, or taking your own, is a better option for those who want to see something of Corsica's diverse landscape and attractions.

Travelling around Sardinia, on the other hand, is much easier. Though the island is also mountainous, its roads are, on the whole, much less tortuous, and a surprising number of them are in good condition, though petrol stations and refreshment halts are infrequent, so it is wise to be prepared.

While Corsica possibly has the edge over Sardinia in respect of extremely attractive little holiday resorts and magnificent mountain scenery, the Italian island probably scores over its neighbour when it comes to hotel standards and cuisine. Sardinia's Costa Smeralda, or Emerald Coast, for example, contains some really excellent luxury hotels – the type of establishment that Corsica as yet lacks. Indeed, Corsican hotels, while clean, comfortable and quite well equipped, are generally in the one or two star category, without the type of amenities and facilities that many holidaymakers, weened on the gigantic hotel complexes of the Spanish Costas, with their Olympic-size swimming pools, children's play areas, discothèques and the like, have come to expect. Even four-star establishments in Corsica are relatively thin on the ground, and while the simpler, unsophisticated and sometimes fairly basic type of hotel is just what many holidaymakers are looking for, it does not suit everyone, especially couples with young children.

In Sardinia, run-of-the-mill hotels also tend towards the unsophisticated, but the island does boast a greater number of international-standard properties than its neighbour, not only in the jet-set playground of the Costa Smeralda but in other up-and-coming resort areas.

Likewise, Corsica has nothing, as yet, to match the type of family facilities and amenities offered at Sardinia's Forte village near the resort of Santa Margherita di Pula, virtually a resort-within-a-resort. Again, it is not everyone's cup of tea, but it is certainly extremely popular with British holidaymakers, particularly couples with young children.

Cuisine is another aspect on which Sardinia arguably scores over its neighbour, though I doubt if the Corsicans would agree with me. Corsican cuisine, most will admit, stands little comparison with that of mainland France, neither in terms of variety of ingredients (understandable since much of the produce has to be imported), nor in imaginative cooking, presentation, or sheer flair. Similarly, 'local' cuisine is becoming much more difficult to find, many restaurateurs opting, instead, for the pizza-and-pasta style of operation that does not match up to that of Corsica's Italian neighbour.

Where Corsica certainly steals a march over Sardinia is in the quantity and quality of its camp sites. There are literally hundreds throughout the island, usually very attractively located and many with excellent facilities. Not surprisingly, they are extremely popular with the more budget-minded tourists keen to sample Corsica's beautiful scenery but without the high cost of hotel accommodation.

Thus, from attractive camp sites to picturesque coastal resorts and superb family hotels, the islands of Corsica and Sardinia offer the visitor a truly memorable holiday. As the ensuing chapters will show, both are different in numerous respects . . . but they both extend a warm welcome to the visitor looking for sun, sea, sand, relaxation and interest, all in idyllic surroundings. So, bon voyage – or buon viaggio!

CORSICA – AN INTRODUCTION

'Empty my head of Corsica! Empty it of honour, empty it of humanity,
empty it of friendship, empty it of piety. No! while I live, Corsica and the
cause of the brave islanders shall ever employ my attention, shall ever
interest me in the sincerest manner.'

JAMES BOSWELL

CORSICA IS A beautiful island and an astonishingly diverse one. It is
crowned by spectacular mountain peaks that fold and fall away into
ravines and valleys, with pine forests stretching below the snow
line, the scented maquis fleecing the slopes, and vines ripening on
the rolling hills to make robust Corsican wines. It is an island
veined with rivers, rushing headlong into waterfalls, chasing fat
trout; and in the midst of the mountain greenery, little red-roofed
towns with their distinctive church bell-towers cling like barnacles
to impossible sites, and ancient citadels, such as Corte and Sartène,
harbour the secrets of centuries.

Corsica is a paradise for holiday makers, with a thousand
kilometres of superb coastline – golden beaches, coves, gulfs and
mountains rising sheer from the sea. Holiday activities include
sailing, fishing, climbing, skin-diving in the limpid waters around
Cap Corse, canoeing in mountain rivers, skiing at Vergio and
Haut-Asco, or simply relaxing on a beach of fine, pale golden
sand.

Geographically the island divides diagonally into two: steep
mountain country to the northwest, with Monte Cinto the highest
peak; and to the southeast more mountains, gradually descending
to the east-coast plains and the stratified cliffs of Bonifacio in the
extreme south.

Between the two halves runs the spectacular
Ajaccio-Corte-Bastia main road and, equally spectacular, but
more restful, the railway. Both pass secretive old towns, forests of
oak, chestnut and fragrant pine, gorges with raging torrents, and
upland pastures where cattle, sheep, goats and pigs roam at will.
Here the air is scented with resin, crystal water bubbles out of
springs, and wild strawberries, raspberries, mulberries,
mushrooms, cyclamen and pale-green hellebore flourish according

11

to the season. In winter, deep in snow, the forests are silent and unbelievably beautiful.

In the plains the once-prevalent malaria has been eradicated. The maquis, a dense undergrowth whose fire risk is a constant threat to the forests, has been brought under control; vineyards, orchards and early vegetables now contribute to the island's economy.

Corsica's spectacular mountains form a glorious backdrop to a series of delightful holiday resorts, each with its own character, its own picturesque setting, its own kind of beach whether a ribbon of sand or a rocky cove of fine shale.

Holidaying in Corsica is both simple and sophisticated. You can feel close to nature, yet have all the convenience of civilization . . . splendid harbours and marinas, watersports galore, little restaurants where you can savour local specialities such as cured hams, salty brocciu cheese and freshly caught fish. Add to all this a range of adequate if not super-luxurious hotels, self-catering and camping options, and who could ask for much more?

Tourism in Corsica is a comparatively recent phenomenon, concentrated round the tiny fishing villages of the coast, especially the west coast, and further depopulating the interior, except when expatriate Corsicans return for summer family reunions. Fine beaches and the Mediterranean climate have attracted increasing crowds over the last 20 years, and holiday accommodation is now crammed to capacity every July and August. French and Italian visitors predominate, but an increasing number of British, too, are discovering the wild beauty of the island, and its excellent little holiday resorts, which now attract about 1,100,000 holidaymakers a year.

Development is still low-key, the cost of importing materials and consumer goods being high, and holidays in Corsica are more expensive than many competing holiday destinations, though on a par with Sardinia. French cuisine is not one of the imports. While adequate and tasty, food in the resorts is often fairly basic, standard international fare – steak, spaghetti, ice cream. Fish is varied but expensive. Corsican food includes game in season, sheep and goat cheese, chestnut-flavoured sweetmeats, paté made from blackbirds and pigeons and a variety of charcuterie from the island's small native pigs – hams, smoked fillets, sausages made from pigs' liver. Wines range from fruity whites to powerful reds, and there are local eaux-de-vie and liqueurs.

Unless you are content to stay on your idyllic beach, you need a car for exploring. Public transport is limited, and coach trips inadequate for the lure of the magnificent mountain and coastal scenery. Roads inland are plentiful, but driving is a test of skill and patience: even the central artery from Ajaccio through Corte to Bastia has its steep hairpin bends, and the smaller, narrow roads are continually hair-raising, while Corsicans seem to drive with the venom once reserved for vendettas. Distances have nothing to do with how the crow flies – the tourist must crawl with caution, and on a long excursion it is wise to carry spare petrol.

Buses are infrequent and expensive, unlike on Sardinia, and hotels much less common and more expensive than on the mainland; neither are they, on the whole, particularly sophisticated, with a few notable exceptions. However, even with their high prices they tend to be fully booked in high season, so advance reservations are strongly recommended. Camping, though, is an ideal option, and there are scores of well-equipped camping sites throughout the island; in this respect it is much better served than Sardinia. The Corsican government has banned unofficial camping in the belief that it is a cause of brush fires as well as a source of tension between locals and tourists, but on my last visit there was little evidence of the ban being observed, and some of the most staggeringly beautiful mountain sites were almost ruined by piles of litter deposited by the sides of the mountain roads by thoughtless 'unofficial campers.'

For those who enjoy boating, Corsica is a haven for navigators in very kind of vessel, from yachts to inflatable dinghies. The rocky, jagged coastline invites exploration among inlets and beaches inaccessible to landlubbers. Especially attractive are Cap Corse, the Agriates Desert, the bays of Girolata and Porto, and the southern coast of Propriano, Bonifacio and Porto-Vecchio. Among the best-equipped marinas are Ajaccio, Propriano, Porto-Vecchio, Campoloro, Macinaggio, Centuri-Port, Saint-Florent, Sant' Ambroggio and Calvi.

For those who like stay-put holidays there is an enormous choice, while for visitors who prefer to be on the move the island offers unending variety. The energetic can ramble on foot, following trails or marked footpaths, or on horseback, trekking from Venaco, Calacuccia, Serra de Scopamene and Zonza; one can travel by train, or car, through some of the most awe-inspiring scenery imaginable.

Like Sardinia, Corsica is basically a summer holiday destination as opposed to a year-round one. Indeed, despite the efforts of the local tourism authorities to extend the season into spring and early winter, the vast majority of hotels and restaurants throughout the island open up only in late May and close for the winter at the end of September. Thus the majority of holidaymakers the island attracts are concentrated into the months of July and August.

The scent of Corsica is rightly famous. Such a heady welcome awaits you as you step from your plane that, even if you were blindfolded, you would still know you were in Corsica.

If you are fond of beaches there are scores from which to choose: wide, sweeping, majestic beaches; tiny, secluded beaches where you will only be disturbed by, or disturb, crabs and birds; sea temperatures are good and the water is clean.

Corsica is a location of landscapes, each with its own characteristics. In the north-east, rugged grey rock forms the long spine of Cap Corse and the complex relief of the Castagniccia's ridges and valleys. The larger central mountain mass is many-coloured granite in giant tilted blocks; powerful rivers have gouged out valleys through the parallel ridges, and erosion has produced dramatic distorted configurations. In the west the ridges slope to a coast of bays and promontories; to the east they drop down to a flat plain behind a much straighter shoreline. There are Alpine pastures among the high central peaks, above slopes of magnificent pines; lower down are rich chestnut forests and fertile valleys where vines, olives and orchards flourish.

For centuries the Corsicans retreated inland from their invaded coasts. They lived in mountain communes, shepherding huge flocks up and down according to the season, farming land only to provide for minimal needs and building from local materials the villages which vary so attractively from region to region. Poverty, pride and what amounted to imprisonment in their own country produced both lethargy and the high tension of internal vendettas, not dissimilar to those in Sardinia. Those who could went abroad. But despite their resentment at being handed over to the French, Corsicans took full advantage of their new status: Napoléon himself was among the first to benefit from French education and opportunities for advancement. The island grew even poorer and more neglected as its younger talent departed to careers in France, particularly in the police, the army and the colonial service. After the Second World War much coastal land was cleared of its malarial mosquitoes, but government grants to develop Corsican agriculture chiefly benefited immigrants from Algeria, able and willing to apply modern methods to farming the fertile eastern plain.

14

RECOMMENDED HOLIDAY RESORTS

Corsica is not a cheap holiday destination, and package tours incorporating even fairly basic hotel or holiday village accommodation are fairly expensive when compared with many other holiday islands and Mediterranean resorts. However, it does boast an enormous choice of extremely attractive and well-equipped resorts to cater for most tastes and preferences, and holiday costs can be reduced by seeking out good, but less sophisticated hotels, or opting for camping, while numerous self-catering flats and studios also offer a good alternative.

AJACCIO

Ajaccio, the island's 'capital', is understandably busy, bustling and lively. It has a good range of hotels in the town itself – though these can be noisy, especially at the height of the season – and there are literally scores of restaurants, cafes, discothèques, bars, cinemas, museums and the like, together with an excellent beach of fine sand, making Ajaccio ideal for holidaymakers who enjoy a beach but also want interesting alternatives.

PORTICCIO

For those who do not enjoy 'big town' atmosphere, and instead prefer that of the purpose-built holiday resorts where the emphasis is on the beach and its attendant activities, the resort of Porticcio, round the bay from Ajaccio, has much to commend it. The beach itself is excellent, and the facilities developed alongside it, such as hotels, holiday villages, camp sites, restaurants, cafés and boutiques, are of a very high standard.

One slight disadvantage is that, being quite close to Ajaccio's airport of Campo dell'Oro, the tranquillity of the setting, not surprisingly, is sometimes disturbed by the roar of jet aircraft ferrying holidaymakers to and from the island. Ajaccio, however, is not London or New York, and flights are not exactly taking off or landing every few minutes.

PROPRIANO

Further down the coast from Ajaccio and Porticcio, and consequently further away from the airport, is another small, fairly new holiday resort, Propriano, developed from a tiny fishing port and offering a selection of smallish hotels both grouped round a picturesque yachting harbour and also situated on the road leading out of the resort. Facilities are good, and Propriano is an excellent choice for those looking for a quieter holiday resort, without the larger choice of nighttime distractions offered at many of the island's bigger holiday centres.

CALVI

Of all Corsica's holiday resorts, Calvi probably takes some beating. Not only does it boast a superb beach, but the town itself is picturesque in the extreme, with an ancient citadel, attractive old houses, restaurants by the score, and an excellent range of hotels. For those looking for a beach holiday combined with a splendid range of amusements and entertainments, in a delightful setting, Calvi would be my firm recommendation.

ST-FLORENT

The picturesque port and holiday resort of St-Florent, likewise, has a great deal to offer the holidaymaker, though with a large, yet extremely attractive pleasure port crammed with yachts and motor cruisers, the emphasis here is rather more on the boating fraternity than on the beach lover. Nevertheless, the bay on which St-Florent is located boasts some excellent beaches, and overall facilities in the resort, such as hotels, restaurants, discothèques, shops and amusements, are of a very high order.

16

ILE-ROUSSE

Ile-Rousse is one of Corsica's oldest holiday resorts, and though efforts have been made of late to spruce the place up to compete with 'upstarts' such as Propriano, Porticcio and the like, including the recent creation of a small but attractive promenade between the central square and beach, the resort retains a somewhat traditional and conservative air, and remains particularly popular with slightly older holidaymakers.

PORTO-VECCHIO

Unlike Ile-Rousse, Porto-Vecchio is today catering for both the younger holidaymakers and for the yachting fraternity, thanks to the expansion of its pleasure port and the recent development of numerous attractive new hotels, campsites and holiday villages on or near its very pretty bay. The town itself enjoys a magnificent setting, and its highly picturesque streets are crammed with delightful little restaurants and cafés.

PORTO-POLLO

Of the smaller, newly-developed coastal resorts, Porto-Pollo is arguably one of the best – and is certainly one of the most attractive. The beach is extensive though narrow, and while facilities are somewhat limited by international-resort standards, with only a few simple and unsophisticated hotels, a couple of restaurants and the like, it is a lovely spot for those looking for a quiet beach holiday away from the masses and the discothèques.

CENTURI-PORT

Finally, there is the tiny fishing port of Centuri, one of the most unusual and picturesque in Corsica; it is unsophisticated, relatively unspoilt, and truly delightful.

There are many other pleasant resorts, both large and small, scattered throughout the island, some ideal for stay-put holidays and others, like Bonifacio – which does not have a beach of its own, although there are excellent ones nearby – more suited, in my view, to day visits.

AJACCIO

Tucked into the north-west corner of the beautiful gulf of the same name, and the arrival point for many visitors by both air and sea, Ajaccio has been described by some writers as a rather haphazard version of Cannes. But while it may lack the sophistication and style of its mainland cousin, it does have considerable appeal, sweetened as it is by the waters of the Prunelli river which cascade down from Monte Renoso, framed by the mass of Monte d'Oro, one of the island's highest peaks, and dominated by a citadel built by the French.

A relatively new town, founded in 1492, the year when Christopher Colombus, claimed to be a Corsican from Calvi (a claim disputed by the Genoese, among others) discovered America, Ajaccio was originally called Agiation by the Greeks, then Adjacium by the Romans, and developed along a beautiful bay in what probably was the present Saint Jean district, where traces of the Roman occupation and a paleochristian basilica have been discovered.

The present name of Ajaccio is mentioned in the letters of Saint Gregoire le Grand, who was Pope in 600 AD, and we are told that the inhabitants welcomed Alphonse of Aragon in 1420 before the Genoese granted special privileges to the town. An epidemic, almost certainly malaria, struck the town, and in 1492 the few inhabitants who had been spared decided to settle 2 km to the west, on the Capo di Bollo peninsula.

The republic of Genoa sent 100 Ligurian families to settle in the new town, whose boundaries are now the square Fesch (formerly known as Piazza d'Olmo and subsequently Place des Palmiers), Quai Napoléon, Boulevard Lantivy, Boulevard Eugene Macchini and Avenue 1er Consul. A castle was built where the citadel now stands, and the town was encircled by high defensive walls whose construction was completed in 1503; the original gates were at the entrance to the present rue Bonaparte. Ajazzo, as the town was then known, was thus strongly guarded against Barbaresque pirates, who for centuries ravaged the Mediterranean coasts.

In 1553 the French, under the command of Maréchal de Termes, took the town with the help of Sampiero Corso and the Turkish fleet of Admiral Draguth. The town received considerable improvements from King Henry II, the walls being repaired and improved and a stronghold built round the castle. In 1559, as a result of the Treaty of Cambressis, the King of France was obliged to give Corsica back to the Genoese, and observers considered it was a loss more important than those of Parma or Sinna.

For a long period Ajaccio remained principally a Genoese city and Corsicans had to settle on the other side of Piazza d'Olmo. This built-up area called le Borgo (suburb) became first rue Sainte-Catherine, then rue Fesch. By the end of the 17th century the houses had not reached the small church of Saint-Roch.

In 1656, when the Black Death raged through Italy, the town of Ajaccio was taken under the protection of the 'miraculous Virgin of Savona,' Our Lady of Mercy. The town was apparently saved, and the Virgin became its patron saint, from which time Our Lady of Mercy is feasted each year on March 18.

During the Forty Year War Corsicans tried to free themselves from the Genoese yoke. In 1769 the French, under the command of Général de Vaux, took possession of Corsica; the island became part of the French realm and from then on its destiny became that of France. The same year, Napoléon Bonaparte was born in the town, and over the last 200 years or so its population has increased from 5,000 in the 18th century, when it was described as the prettiest little town in the Mediterranean, to a built-up area of 60,000 inhabitants.

Although undistinguished for its architectural splendours or art treasures, despite being the capital of Corsica, Ajaccio's streets and squares are dignified and pleasantly lined by palm trees, and there is no lack of the picturesque off the main throughfares, where narrow, arched streets are lined by huge houses each one a potential fortress.

The town is understandably proud of its most famous son, and every second bar, street, restaurant, café and public building is named Napoléon, or Bonaparte, or 'le petit caporal' while, least we forget or miss the point, there are several statues of the Emperor dotted about the place.

The Chapel Impériale, built in 1855 on the orders of Napoléon III, is another of Prince Victor's gifts to the nation. Here rest nine Bonapartes and the tombs of seven, including Napoléon's father and mother and of Cardinal Fesch himself.

In Ajaccio's streets three statues ensure that one does not forget that this indeed is the 'Imperial' city. Largest and most ambitious is on the principal square, the Place Général de Gaulle, known before 1945 as Place du Diamont. Based on a design by Viollet-le-Duc, restorer of Avignon's ramparts, it represents Napoléon on horseback, framed by his four brothers in togas.

On the Place du Maréchal Foch, Napoléon, accompanied by four lions, is shown as First Consul, this time wearing a toga. Finally, on the Place D'Austerlitz, at the western end of the Boulevard Général Leclerc, is a modern statue of Napoléon by Seurre, unveiled in 1938 on the 169th anniversary of his birth. It is a replica of that which stood on the Colonne Vendome in Paris until 1863 and is now to be found in Les Invalides. The emperor is depicted here in his famous redingote, the familiar bicorne on his head, hand in waistcoat, and staring out to sea.

As well as the Napoléonic reminders, Ajaccio has much to offer the visitor. The Musée Fesch, for example, is of particular interest to lovers of early Italian painting. The splendid collection it houses owes its existence to the magpie instincts of Napoléon's step-uncle, Cardinal Fesch, son of Napoléon's maternal grandmother and a Swiss officer in the Genoese army.

Its best works include the Mystic Marriage of Catherine by the Umbrian Allegretto Nuzy (14th century), the Virgin of the Garland by Botticelli (1470), the Madonna and two Saints by Cosme Tura, also 15th century, as well as the Man with a Glove by Titian and Leda by Veronese – two marvellous 16th century works. Below the museum, on the ground floor, is the library, founded by Lucian Bonaparte when Minister of the Interior in 1800 and in which an estimated 50,000 volumes are housed.

Ajaccio's cathedral, the work of Giacomo della Porta, architect of Pope Gregory XIII, was begun in 1554 but was not completed until 1593. It boasts a magnificent Delacroix, Vièrge du Sacre Coeur, in the first chapel to the left, built by Pietro-Paulo d'Ornano to the memory of his only son.

The white marble high altar was a gift of Napoléon's sister, Elisa Bacciocchi, while to the right of the main entrance is the white marble font which was used on the occasion of his baptism. In the second chapel to the right is a medallion offered by Madame Mère as a thanksgiving for her son's great victory at Montenotte; to the left a plaque commemorating Napoléon's words a few days before his death in May 1821 . . . 'If my dead body is proscribed as my living person has been, I would wish to be buried beside my forbears in the Cathedral of Ajaccio in Corsica.'

The heart of Ajaccio is the Cours Grandval, prolonged to the west by the Boulevard Général Lecler, to the east by the Avenue de Paris and the Avenue Premier Consul, and like main streets of many Mediterranean towns, it abounds with cafés and shops.

Leading off the cours Grandval are numerous picturesque little streets and alleys containing the cream of Ajaccio's restaurants. Some, like Da Mamma, specialising in Corsican cuisine. Nightlife is pretty lively, too, with the Dolce Vita and the Palm Beach being among the most popular nightclub/discothèques. For a traditional evening there are more classical places where you can sing along to local musicians and, while the tunes may not always be strictly Corsican, they are great fun.

Unlike many other resorts and towns in Corsica, where public transport is poor, Ajaccio does have a relatively good bus service, and is the starting point for a spectacular train journey.

The Bay of Ajaccio is comparable in beauty to the Bay of Naples, with encircling mountains presenting a majestic backdrop to the sea, and inlets, beaches and natural anchorage make this one of the most popular holiday spots on the island.

Along the cliff road, hewn from the granite around the bay, villas and luxury hotels stand incongruously next to the grandiose funerary chapels that face the roads and highways. The beaches of Scudo and Vignola offer superb aquatic sports.

Beyond the airport at Campo dell'Oro the southern coast of the bay of Ajaccio has been extensively developed for tourism, with Porticcio, across from Ajaccio, being the focal point of seafront development.

PLACES OF INTEREST

Napoléonic Museum, Town Hall, 1st Floor
Displayed in the rooms of the Town Hall, it houses paintings, and genealogy and documents of the Imperial Age as well as a collection of medals dating from the 1st Empire.

Open every day except Sundays from 0.900 to 12.00 hours and 14.00 to 17.00 hours.

Maison Bonaparte, rue Saint-Charles

In 1769 the Bonaparte family occupied the lower two floors of this house, with a family called Pozzo di Borgo living above them. Under the English occupation from 1793 to 1796 the house was occupied by British troops, and it is said that Hudson Lowe, Napoléon's future gaoler on the island of Sainte-Helena, lodged here for a while.

Today the house is a museum open from 09.00 to 12.00 and 14.00 to 17.00 hours. One can see various relics and curiosities, including the bedroom of Madame Letizia in which she brought Napoléon into the world.

EXCURSIONS

Walks into the hills beyond Ajaccio lead to magnificent panoramas. From Ajaccio visits can be made by both road and boat to the Iles Sanguinaires; alternatively, the southern borders of the Gulf of Ajaccio offer a panoramic circuit along the coast to Porticcio and Chiavari, and an inland return route via the Col d'Aja Bastiano. The railway gives an opportunity for the individualist to pass a day in the mountains and forests around Vizzavona, or exploring the fortress town of Corte.

A further excursion in the vicinity of Ajaccio is to the Château de la Punta, set in large grounds and commanding views both of the coast and inland to Monte o'Orbo and Monte Renoso.

A longer excursion is to the Calanche de Piana, near Porto, where the red granite cliffs falling several hundred feet to the sea are awe-inspiring.

FETES AND FESTIVALS

18 March: Festival of Our Lady of Mercy, patron saint of the town
Good Friday: Religious procession through the streets
5 May: Mass commemorating the death of Emperor Napoléon, celebrated in the Impérial Chapel
2 June: Religious procession through the town in honour of the patron saint of fishermen, Saint Erasmus

USEFUL ADDRESSES

TOURIST INFORMATION
Agence Regionale du Tourisme et des Loisirs, 22 Cours Grandval,
  tel. 95510022
Office de Tourism, Hôtel de Ville, tel. 95214087

HOTELS
Hotel du Palais, 5 Av Beverini, tel. 9523364
Costa, Blvd Colomba 2, tel. 95214302
Albion, Av Gal-Leclerc 15, tel. 95216670
Napoléon, Rue Lorenzo-Vero 4, tel. 95213001
Hotel Columba, 2 Av de Paris, tel. 95211266
Belvedere, 4 Rue Henry-Dunant, tel. 95210726

HOLIDAY VILLAGE
Club des Calanques, tel. 95520234

CAMPING
Pech Baretta, tel. 95520117

RESTAURANTS
Chez Pardi, 6 Rue Fesch, tel. 95214308
U Focone, 1 Rue Général-Campi, tel. 95211385
Da'Mamma, Passage de la Guingette, tel. 952213944
L'Amore Piattu, Place du Gal-de-Gaulle 8, tel. 95510053
Côte d'Azur, Cours Napoléon 12, tel. 95215024

CLUB
Casino, Blvd Lantivy, tel. 9521414

CABARETS
Pavilion Bleu, Av Général-Leclerc
Au Son des Guitares, rue roi-de-Rome

DISCOTHÈQUES
Le Palm Beach, rte des Sanguinaires, tel. 95213562
Dolce Vita, rte des Sanguinaires, tel. 95213520

CINEMAS
L'Empire, Cours Napoléon 28
Laetivia, Cours Napoléon 22

CAR HIRE
Avis, 3 Place de Gaulle, tel. 952100186; Blvd Sampiero,
tel. 95214360; airport, tel. 95232514
Balesi, 4 Rue Emmanuel-Arène, tel. 95210611; airport,
tel. 95232129
Carli, Le Chypre, résidence des Iles, tel. 05214910
Casavia, airport, tel. 95232318
Castellani, airport, tel. 95232219
Corsorto, airport, tel. 95233593
Citer, airport, tel. 95227611
Europcar, 16 Cours Grandval, tel. 95210549; airport,
tel. 95231593
Hertz, 8 Cours Grandval, tel. 95217094; airport, tel. 95232417
Inter Rent, 5 montée St-Jean, tel. 95226179

BOAT HIRE
S.A.A.G. Loisirs 19, Cours Prince-Impérial, tel. 2125520
Thalasso, Tahiti Beach, tel. 220158
Europ Yachting, Quai de la Citadelle, tel. 210057
Reybier, Quai de la Citadelle
Voile et Loisirs, 9 rue Roi de Rome, tel. 215765
Centre Nautique de Porticcio, Plage de la Viva, tel. 250106
Hexa Voile, Quai de la Citadelle, tel. 216401

NAUTICAL CLUBS
Société Nautique d'Ajaccio, 'Le Golfe,' Quai de la Citadelle,
tel. 95213575
A.S.P.T.T. Ajaccio, Plage du Ricanto, tel. 223807
Centre de Formation et de Perfectionnement Nautique d'Ajaccio,
Port de la Citadelle, tel. 95210779

SKIN DIVING
Subaqua-Club de Porticcio, Plage de la Viva, tel. 95250603
Possidonia-Club, 22 rue Diena
Sub-Aquasport d'Ajaccio, résidence des Iles immeuble la
Majorque, rte des Sanguinaires, tel. 95510606
Club de Plongée de l'Amiraute, Amiraute, tel. 95202679

TRAVEL AGENCIES
Auto-Excursions Ollandini, 3 Place de Gaulle, tel. 95210186
Publitour, 6 rue Fesch, tel. 95210664 and 95216880
Corstourisme, 5 Place Foch, tel. 95212960

Imperial Tours, 6 Diamant II, Place de Gaulle, tel. 95216848
Havas, 1 Av de 1er Consul, tel. 95214966
Corsica Vacances, 13 Rue Maréchal Ornano, tel. 95214339
Sarrola Tourisme, 15 Blvd Sampiero, tel. 95231101
Société des Autocars de l'Ile de Beauté, 4 Av de Paris,
   tel. 95215374

POLICE
Ajaccio Gendarmerie, tel. 95210826/95232036

HOSPITAL
Centre Hospitalier, Av Impératrice Eugénie, tel. 95211500

HORSE RIDING
Cercle Hippique Ajaccien, tel. 95221622
Eperon de Zalla, tel. 95214786
Poney Club, Centre de Randonnées Equestres, tel. 95230310

TENNIS
Le Casone, tel. 95211229
Les Milelli, rte d'Alata, tel. 95232344
Tennis-Club de Mezzavia, col Stiletto, tel. 95201408
La Parata, tel. 95520025

GO-KART RACING
Sarrola Karting, 12 km from Ajaccio, on the Sarrola-Carcopino
   Road.

TAXIS
Station Place Général-de-Gaulle, tel. 95210087
Station Av Pascal Paoli, tel. 95232570
Station Palais de Justice, tel. 95232570

BANKS
Banque de France, 8 Rue du Sergent-Casalonga, tel. 95210005
Banque Populaire Provençale et Corse, 6 Av Antoine Sérafini,
   tel. 95214985
Société Générale, 4 rue Sergent-Casalonga, tel. 95214130

RAIL STATION, tel. 95231103

POST OFFICE, Cours Napoléon, tel. 95211360

AIRPORT, Campo dell'Oro, tel. 95210770

BUS STATION, Quai l'Herminier, part of the Gare Maritime,
tel. 95212801

FERRIES
SNCM, Quai l'Herminier, tel. 95219070

MEDICAL EMERGENCY, tel. 95215050

Aléria

Aléria, on the east coast of Corsica, has been earmarked for
considerable touristic development, with proposals for a golf
course among many new amenities. The resort's beach itself is
currently relatively underdeveloped, apart from a couple of
make-shift beach bars and a three-star camping site, but it seems
only a matter of time before all that will change, with Aléria
destined to become one of the island's top resorts.

Aléria was the ancient capital of Corsica by virtue of its strategic
position straddling sea routes to the eastern Mediterranean.
Known as Alalia to the Greeks who founded it in about 56 BC, it
prospered through trade with Greece, Italy, Sicily, Gaul, Spain
and Carthage. In 259 BC the Romans took Alalia to use as their
base of operations for the colonisation of Corsica.

PLACES OF INTEREST

MUSEUM
Housed in 12 rooms of a Genoese fort built in 1572, it contains a
permanent display of archaeological finds from ancient Alalia,
such as funerary relics, weapons and ceramics. The entrance ticket
to the museum also covers the Roman excavations which have
revealed a forum, temple, baths and law courts.

NEARBY
The lagoon of Diana, renowned for its oysters; and the interesting
mountain villages of Campi and Topx, the latter with many
fascinating 15th century houses.

USEFUL ADDRESSES

TOURIST INFORMATION
Mairie, tel. 95570073

HOTEL
Les Orangers, tel. 95570031

HOLIDAY VILLAGE
Village de Casabianca, tel. 95570689

CAMPING
Marina d'Aleria, tel. 95570142

NATURIST VILLAGE
Riva Bella, tel. 95388110

HORSE RIDING
Club des 2 Etangs, Domaine de Casabianca, tel. 95570002

BANK
Crédit Agricole, tel. 95570022 and 95570222

Algajola

Algajola is a mainly modern, unsophisticated resort, set on a long
sandy beach, with small, simple hotels. The town has a decided
military air, with severe houses and ruined ramparts, erected in
1664 to defend the inhabitants against the Saracens who had
already paid one visit in 1643. The citadel was constructed in the
17th century alongside a fortified castle which was the residence of
the lieutenant-gouverneur of the Balagne. Also of interest is the
church of St-Georges, notable for its tiny, high windows, and
interesting painting attributed to a 17th century Italian artist.

    From Algajola there is easy access to the resorts of Calvi and
Ile-Rousse on the little railway line that runs along this part of the
coast. Close by, the tiny Marine de St-Ambroggio has self-catering
complexes and villas, a Club Med. village, watersports and several
small sandy beaches.

USEFUL ADDRESSES

HOTELS
Tepina Village, tel. 607022
Stella Mare, tel. 607118
De la Plage, tel. 607212

HOLIDAY VILLAGE
Ashra-Hotel Chantilly, tel. 95607042

CAMPING
Cala di Sole, tel. 95607398
De la Plage, tel. 95607176

RESTAURANTS
California, rte du Port, tel. 95600113
Chez Pancrace (Osteria Porte Suprane), evenings only

BOAT HIRE
Corse Méditerranée Mer Services, tel. 95607074

Asco

The village of Asco, located in the valley of the same name at the mouth of the river gorge, is the only village in the valley, and attracts hunters, anglers, botanists and climbers lured by the promise of an away-from-it-all holiday in delightful surroundings. The river Asco winds through the austere but magnificent landscape of the highest mountains in Corsica, while rugged snow-capped peaks exceeding 2,000 metres in altitude, pine woods, granite walls channelling the torrent, and a low scrub-covered valley, add to the variety and diversity of the landscape.

The Asco valley subsists on a mountain economy based on forestry and livestock, and is the habitat of the bearded vulture, an endangered species with a wing span exceeding 2.5 m. Wild sheep are protected in a nature reserve in the upper valley.

Haut-Asco is popular with skiers from December to April, and in summer it becomes a base camp for mountaineers' assaults on

Mount Cinto. Honey from the region is particularly prized.

Ascans claim to be of pure Ligurian stock, true Corsicans whose blood has never been polluted by that of the island's many invaders.

Much of the region falls within the Corsica National Park, which covers about 150,000 hectares, and is the habitat of lynx, deer and wild boar, among other animals and wildlife species.

USEFUL ADDRESSES

HOTEL
Chalet du Haut Asco, tel. 95478108

Balagne

The Balagne is a delightful green and fertile area of wooded hills, lush valleys and many charming villages, threaded with little roads and ideal for leisurely touring. Throughout Corsica's history her invaders have enjoyed this region: the Romans first cultivated it, the Moors in the Middle Ages left some flat-roofed cubic villages among the more characteristic red tiles and huddled grey walls, and the Papal forces who expelled the Moors built scores of pretty churches. This 'garden of Corsica' flourished like nowhere else in the island, growing olives, oranges, figs and almonds as well as the vines which still produce good wine.

As the coast developed it grew rather neglected and depopulated, but there was a revival in the 1960s based on local crafts such as woodcarving, pottery, baskets and, more recently, glass.

Among the most attractive villages in the region are Zilia, Speloncato, Lumio and Montemaggiore, while the hamlet of Pigna is a thriving centre both of crafts and of local gastronomic specialities.

Endowed with a climate in which palms and Barbary figs still flourish, Balagne has also succeeded in developing its coastline for tourism. Popular resorts include Calvi, Algajola, Ile-Rousse, the marina at Sant' Ambroggio and an extensive holiday village at Lozari, stretching over 50 acres along a beautiful sandy beach.

Bastelica

A favourite summer excursion from Ajaccio, being surrounded by delightful walks and climbs, Bastelica was the birthplace of Corsican hero Sampiero Corso in 1498. During an heroic career he succeeded in briefly liberating Corsica from Genoese rule, but was betrayed and murdered by relatives of his late wife whose murder Sampiero had arranged for suspected treason and infidelity.

A bronze statue of Sampiero brandishing a sword is to be found on a large pedestal in front of the church of Santo, most important of Bastelica's several hamlets, and three faces of the pedestal bear ornamentation evoking the combats fought between Corsicans and Genoese.

Also of interest is the house in which Sampiero was born in the hamlet of Dominicacci. Destroyed by the Genoese, it was restored in the 18th century, and carries an inscription prepared in 1855 by William Wyse.

Nearby is the Prunelli Gorge, reached through the village of Tolla, where the houses overlook a reservoir; and Mount Renoso, at 2,352 metres one of the most dramatic lookout points on the island.

Bastia

Holidaymakers arriving at Bastia by air or sea tend to take one look at the town and flee, for there can be no denying that it lacks the charm of many other Corsican towns, and even the sandy beaches on the outskirts, which have been developed into small resorts, do not have the scenic appeal of many other resorts on the island.

However, behind is busy, uninspiring streets, Bastia does have much to offer, its older quarters in particular having a lively atmosphere, while beyond the modern harbour the restaurants and cafés lining the vast tree-shaded Place St-Nicolas, the town's social centre, are animated day and night.

The first settlement was a small fishing village, situated at the mouth of the Guadello stream, which now constitutes the Vieux Port. This settlement, the Marine de Cardo, was a dependent of the hillside village of Cardo, some five kilometres inland, and from such a modest beginning the Genoese transformed the settlement into a military and commercial port, the administrative capital and largest town of the island.

Besides being an excellent strategic location from which to control the Ligurian and Tyrrhenian seas, the Guadello creek offered one of the few natural harbours, however imperfect, between the rocky coastline of Cap Corse to the north, and the inhospitable plain to the south.

The name Bastia derives from bastiglia (a dungeon), indicating that at the outset the settlement was a fortress rather than a town. The site chosen by the Genoese was the promontory flanking the southern shore of the Guadello, offering at once a defensive position, surrounded on three sides by water, and a standpoint from which to command the entrance to the harbour. The dungeon was built here in 1380, protecting the Governor's Palace. As the community in the lee of the bastion grew, so the fortifications were extended until in 1521 the town was completely encompassed by the walls, and the outline of the citadel was established.

The title Terra Nova was bestowed on the fortified town, distinguishing it from the external quartiers which developed outside the walls and in particular around the Vieux Port. The restrictions of the citadel site imposed a high density of building, with narrow streets and few open spaces. The only large public open space today is at the entrance to the citadel in the shadow of the dungeon, the present-day Place du Donjon.

The initial growth of the town outside the citadel was largely as a result of the limited amount of space contained within the walls, legal restrictions limiting Corsican residence within Terra Nova, and also the undesirability of accommodating certain types of land use, such as the cemetery, abbatoirs and gibbet, inside the fortifications. External growth resulted more particularly from the development of the port and the establishment of numerous convents and monasteries.

Under Genoese rule Bastia grew around the Vieux Port, the new streets following the contours in semi-circular fashion, and to the north of the port in the quartier of Terra Vecchia. The defence of these external, unfortified quartiers, was assured by a chain of four hilltop forts that overlooked the entire town. By the middle of the 18th century, the extramuros parts of the town greatly exceeded the walled citadel in area, and the total population of the entire settlement had attained 7,000.

The combined functions of garrison town, commercial port and administrative capital, together with its increasing importance as a regional centre for a productive agricultural hinterland, ensured the supremacy of Bastia during the latter part of the Genoese occupation. After the achievement of independence and incorporation into France, a marked cadence ensued in the rate of growth, and in 1811 Bastia lost its status of island capital to Ajaccio and was reduced to the rank of sous-prefecture; the first half of the 19th century was thus a period of slow progress during which Ajaccio expanded more rapidly in terms of population, public building and transport facilities.

By contrast, the second half of the century witnessed renewed growth during which many of the present features of Bastia appeared, and a new road was engineered to the west of Terra Vecchia, giving improved access to the town, and providing a new north-south axis, the present-day Boulevard Paoli.

During this time the silting up of the Vieux Port, coinciding with the need to improve port facilities to support a new foundry at Toga to the north of Bastia, led to the commencement of work on an artificial harbour. Work began in 1845 on the construction of a massive breakwater sheltering a deep-water harbour adjacent to the Plain of St Nicolas. The construction of the Nouveau Port permitted the reclamation of the waterfront area and the creation of the vast Place St Nicolas. Construction work on the port continued until the close of the century, by which time it had been connected, via a tunnel, to the railway system which was opened in 1888.

To a greater extent than any other Corsican town, Bastia has established substantial suburbs from which there is a daily influx into the town centre. Place St Nicolas is its undisputed geographical and social centre; a handsome open space bordered today by shady avenues of plane trees and palms, and lined on one side by open-air cafés and restaurants. To the east the square overlooks the port, animated by the movements of ferry boats to the continent, and to landward the Boulevard Général-de-Gaulle, with the town's principal restaurants and cafés.

The Vieux Port is Bastia's most colourful area, and is popular with tourists who frequent the cafés, restaurants and nightclubs that flourish around the imposing 17th century church of St Jean Baptiste, whose twin towers overlook the Place de l'Hôtel de Ville, in which the open-air market is the most colourful aspect of the daily scene.

PLACES OF INTEREST

Museum of Corsican Ethnography
Set in the old Palace of Genoese governors, it presents a glimpse of the everyday life and different lifestyles within each region, and explores various customs, costumes and religions. Of particular interest is the room of Underwater Archaeology with its collection of amphoras, while among the exhibits is the turret of the submarine Casabianca, which played a crucial role in the liberation of Corsica during World War II. Open every day from 09.00 to 12.00 and 15.00 to 18.00, with free entrance on Wednesdays.

Cathedral
The cathedral of Ste-Marie was built in 1495 by Mgr Fornari, and is richly decorated.

Church of St Jean Baptiste
The biggest church on the island, this was built in 1636, with two bell towers and a high façade dominating the old port.

Chapel of Ste Croix
This chapel is richly decorated with gilded stucco. The water-blackened image of Christ was found floating in the sea in 1428.

Bibliothèque Municipale
Among the many books housed here is one by Bocaccio printed in Florence in 1527.

Nearby
San Martino di Lota, with the convent of Saint Hyacinthe; the church of Sainte-Lucie, perched on a cliff; the convent of Saint Antoine, containing an impressive wooden tabernacle; and the Oratorie of Monserato.

Excursions
A popular excursion is a tour of Cap Corse, one of the island's showpieces. Bastia is also the starting point for the circuit of the Castagniccia, via the Golo Valley, Ponte-Leccia, Morosaglia and Piedcroce, combining mountain scenery and traditional villages. The railway permits a day excursion to Corte, while public bus services bring the pleasant villages between Bastia and Erbalunga within easy reach.

USEFUL ADDRESSES

TOURIST INFORMATION
35 Blvd Paoli, tel. 95310204; Place St Nicolas, tel. 95310089

HOTELS
Posta Vecchia, Quai des Martyrs, tel. 95323238
Bonaparte, 45 Blvd Gal-Graziani, tel. 95340710

CAMPING
Le Bois de San Damiano, rte de la Marina, tel. 95336802
Les Sables Rouge

RESTAURANTS
Chez Assunta, 4 Place Fontaine-Neuve, tel. 9531670 (a delightful
    redecorated 17th century chapel, serving excellent food)
Bistrot du Port, rue Posta-Vecchia, tel. 95321983
U Tianu, 4 rue Mgr-Rico, tel. 9531667
La Taverna, 9 rue du Gal-Carbuccia, tel. 95311787
La Catina di l'Artigiani, rue St-Michel, La Citadelle, tel. 312467

CABARETS
U Rataghiu, rue Carnot, tel. 95312237
U Fanale, Vieux-Port, Place Galetta, tel. 95326838
Son des Guitares, rue de la Marine, tel. 95323158

DISCOTHÈQUES
L'Odyssee, Quai Sud, Vieux-Port, tel. 95313176
Saint-Nicolas, Place Saint-Nicolas, tel. 95311594
Le Tacot, Place Saint-Nicolas, tel. 953103114
L'Apocalypse, rte de la Marana, tel. 95317146

CINEMAS
Le Regent, rue César-Campinchi
Studio, rue de la Misericorde

TRAVEL AGENCIES
Autocars Bastiais, 4 Blvd Paoli, tel. 310179
Kallistour, 6 Av Maréchal-Sébastiani, tel. 312295
Negroni, Lupino district, tel. 302074 and 314404
Ollandini, 9 Av Maréchal-Sébastiani, tel. 314404
Aquila Tours, 15 Blvd du Général-Graziani, tel. 311716

POST OFFICE
Av Maréchal-Sebastiani

AIRPORT
Bastia-Poretta, 23 km away, tel. 95319931 (buses leave from Place
de la Gare).

CAR HIRE
Avis, 2 rue Notre-Dame-de-Lourdes, tel. 95312584
Alfa Cital, airport, tel. 95360556
Citer, Garage Citroen, route Nationale 193, tel. 95314200; airport,
tel. 95360785
Corsica Auto Location, 11 rue Luce de Casabianca, tel. 95315045;
airport tel. 95360361
Emmanuelli, airport, tel. 95360288
Europcar, 30 rue César-Campinichi, tel. 95315929; airport,
tel. 950360355
Hertz, square Saint-Victor, tel. (95) 311424; airport, tel. 95360246
and 95360021
Solvet, airport, tel. 95360195

SKIN DIVING
Neptune-Club Bastiais, 6 Av Maréchal-Sébastiani, tel. 95316002

HORSE RIDING
Société Hippique Urbaine de Bastia, plaine de Montesoro,
tel. 95311528

POLICE, tel. 95335169

RAIL STATION
Place de la Gare, off Maréchal-Sébastiani, tel. 95326006

FERRIES
SNCM (to France), Hôtel de la Chambre de Commerce,
tel. 95313663
Corsica Ferries (to Italy), 5 bis, rue Chanoine Lewschi,
tel. 95311809
NAV.AR.MA Lines (to Italy), 40 Blvd Paoli, tel. 95310179

TAXIS tel. 95310302

HOSPITAL
Centre Hospitalier, tel. 95312827

BANKS
Bank de France, 2 Cours Pierangeli, tel. 95312409
Crédit Agricole, 13 Blvd du Général-de-Gaulle, tel. 95315845
Crédit Lyonnais, 22 rue César-Campinchi, tel. 95319944
Société Générale, Place Saint-Nicolas, tel. 95319956

BAVELLA PASS

'The great pine forest of Bavella is one of the most wonderfully beautiful sights nature can produce.'

EDWARD MARSH

A drive through the Bavella Pass, or Col de Bavella as it is known, provides probably the most spectacular, if hair-raising, excursion on the island. At an altitude of 1,243 metres, the pass cuts through the Corsal mountain chain, with granite needles rearing above a plateau covered with grass and sparsely strewn with windswept pines. To the north stretches the Incudine Massif, and to the east the sea is framed between walls of red rock.

A good starting-off point is the coastal resort of Solenzara, from which the route crosses Larone Pass, with splendid views, and winds through the attractive Bavella Forest. The small auberge on the pass is an ideal stopping place for refreshments to steady the driver's, and the passengers', nerves, while a little further on is the mountain village of Zonza, with a few simple, unpretentious hotels and restaurants.

Bocognano

The village of Bocognano is set among pines and beautiful chestnut trees. Together with several neighbouring hamlets it formed one of the last bandit strongholds of the island. The Bonelli dynasty, for example, spanned the 19th century. Bonelli Père had three 'wives' and 18 children and controlled acres of valley pasturage. His eldest sons were the blackest of the sheep, with a huge price tag on their heads for many murders. Unbetrayed, and under official amnesty, they raised a company of musketeers and fought in the war of 1870, only to take to the maquis again when it was over. The oldest was caught at the age of 75, but allowed to return to Bocognano where he died in 1912, aged 99, honoured as 'royalty in the maquis.'

Not far from Bocognano is the Scalella Pass, which is narrow, tortuous and steep, but offers superb mountain landscapes . . . gorges twisting on all sides, valleys dropping sheer below, cliffs soaring skyward. it also passes Corsica's highest waterfall, a slim torrent spreading into a wide delicate shimmer named the Bridal Veil, while from the bleak top of the pass there are wonderful views from over the northern peaks.

BONIFACIO

According to Homer's Odyssey, Ulysses sought shelter and rest in Bonfacio just as today, in the summer, many hundreds of tourists do in its harbour area, tucked away in an extraordinary cleft between limestone cliffs and bordered by shops, cafés, and seafood restaurants. Throughout the day the marina is alive with tourists, fishermen and the boating fraternity, while the upper part of the town, set firmly on white limestone, and containing a network of narrow streets within ancient walls, offers striking views to Sardinia.

Bonifacio's setting is extraordinary, with crumbling, creamy bluffs, precipitous and overhung, facing the troubled Sardinian strait, and behind them a long inlet entering from the west: the Goulet de Bonifacio, running parallel to the sea, and completely sheltered. On the narrow promontory the citadel and Haut-Ville rise high, white and seemingly impregnable.

A line of 187 steps scores a 45 degree angle up the rockface from the sea, known as 'The King of Aragon's Staircase,' and said to have been cut by Aragonese soldiers in the course of a single night during an unsuccessful siege in 1420. From the Ville Basse round the port at the eastern end of the inlet it is a steep walk up: there is a road, but it is not open to high-season tourists. Vantage points with breathtaking views are Capo Pertusato to the east, to which you can drive, or the Sol St-Roch up a footpath nearer the encircling ramparts.

Bonifacio reputedly took its name from a Tuscan marquis of the 9th century. It became a pirate stronghold, and the Genoese gained their first foothold in Corsica here only by surprising pirates drunk at a wedding feast; by the late 12th century Bonifacio was a Genoese colony. The whole place is built to resist siege: ramparts immensely thick, grain silos below the Place Grandval, houses

40

designed like mini-fortresses with storage chambers on the ground floor and access originally by ladder to the first. The 'flying buttresses' crossing the cobbled alleys were part of a system of canals and gutters carrying water from a communal cistern under the loggia of the town church. The layout of the promontory town was necessarily compact, a dense little network of streets, shadowed by tall narrow buildings. Today they include cafés and restaurants, craft shops and souvenir shops, while half the site is taken up with the citadel guarding the western point, and today occupied by the French Foreign Legion.

In high season and at fixed hours, visitors are allowed past the guarded gate to visit one of Bonifacio's churches, the Église St-Dominique, built by the Templars at the end of the 13th century in Provençal Gothic style with rare vaulting. The choir was rebuilt in the 18th century, and among many decorative Baroque pieces are two massive religious groups carved in wood, which in true Corsican fashion are carried through the streets in the Easter procession.

The best views of Bonifacio are from the lighthouse at Pertusato on the southern tip of the island (whence Sardinia is visible, only 12 km away), or from the motorboats which take you from the harbour quay on a three quarter of an hour trip round the promontory on which the town was built, passing caves and grottos, the overhanging stratified cliffs, and the steps of the 'Escalier du Roi d'Aragon'. Though Bonifacio itself has no beach, there are sandy beaches within easy driving distance, the nearest being Calalonga and Tonnara.

PLACES OF INTEREST

The citadel, now a base for the French Foreign Legion and closed to visitors.

Church of Ste-Marie Majeure
With its white façade and high, Gothic bell tower, this 15th century church is one of Bonifacio's most striking edifices. Its interior decoration is classic Baroque, and contains a Roman sarcophagus and a beautiful tabernacle dating from 1465.

Nearby
Forty-five minutes by motorboat from the Quai de la Marine are the Marine Caves.

The village of Monacia, 25 km from Bonifaco, has a superb restaurant, La Pergola, tel. 95718142, where you can feast on wild boar.

Cape Pertusato, 5.5 km from Bonifacio, offers a spectacular view of the resort, the islands of Cavallo and Lavezzi, and the Sardinian coast.

Santa Manza Bay, 6 km distant, has rocky inlets and isolated beaches.

USEFUL ADDRESSES

TOURIST INFORMATION
20 rue Longue, tel. 95730348

HOTELS
Solemare, tel. 95730106
La Caravelle, Quai Comparetti, tel. 95730003
Le Centre Nautique, tel. 95730212
Des Etrangers, Av Sylvere Bohn, tel. 95730191

CAMPING
Le Gurgazo, tel. 95730555
Campo di Liccia, tel. 95730309
Araguina, tel. 95730296
Cavallo Morto, tel. 95730499

RESTAURANTS
Stella d'Oro, rue Doria 7, tel. 95730363
L'Anura, Quai Comparetti 14, tel. 95730027
La Semillante, Quai Comparetti 16, tel. 95730834

DISCOTHÈQUES
Au Langoustier, Quai Comparetti, tel. 95730114
U Fragnu, Haute-Ville, tel. 95730044

TRAVEL AGENCY
Ollandini, Quai Comparetti, tel. 95730128

CAR HIRE
Avis, Quai Comparetti, tel. 95730128
Hertz, Marina, tel. 95730247
Europcar, Garage Betti, tel. 95730103

BOAT HIRE
S.C.I.M. Corse, Marina, tel. 95730313 and 95730378

SKIN DIVING
Club de Plongée du Detroit de Bonifacio, tel. 95730273

BANKS
Crédit Lyonnais, 40 rue St Erasme, tel. 95730314
Société Générale, 23 Quai Comparetti, tel. 95730243
Crédit Agricole, tel. 95730276

CROSSINGS TO SARDINIA
Tirrenia sails for the Sardinian port of Santa Teresa, 13 km away, between 1 May and 30 September, three times daily, and twice daily from 1 October to 30 April, the journey taking about 50 minutes.

You can also take a boat from here to La Maddalena, for which there are daily services year-round. Tirrenia's office is open daily from 08.30 to 10.30, and 11.30 to 14.30, and again 15.00 to 17.00.

Sardinia is also served by NAV.AR.A Lines, tel. 95730029, which operates five trips per day from mid-June to mid-September. Their office is open daily from 07.30 to 20.30 hours. All boats leave from the Gare Maritime, at the end of Quai Comparetti, beneath the walls of the upper city, and you can buy your ticket shortly before departure time.

Borgo

Located 19 km from Bastia, the village of Borgo was the scene of the famous victory of Paolists over French troops. Today it offers excellent views over the lagoon of Biguglia, and a Baroque church whose façade carries a plaque commemorating the Paolists' victory.

USEFUL ADDRESSES

HOTEL
Isola, tel. 95331960

HOLIDAY VILLAGE
V.V.F., tel. 95335052

HORSE RIDING
'Cavallu Maranincu, tel. 95360327
Centre Equestre de la Marana, route Lagunaire, tel. 95331676
'Chevaux de San Ornellu,' tel. 95321082

TENNIS
Corsica Country-Club, Hameau Valrose, tel. 95360946

BANK
Crédit Agricole, résidence La Mormorana, tel. 95360182

Bravone

Bravone is situated on the east coast of Corsica and is at the centre
of a series of small resorts which are particularly popular with
naturists, who are catered for in a series of holiday villages and
campsites. Nearby is Aleria, with the excavated remains of an
important Greco-Roman town, and an important museum.

USEFUL ADDRESSES

HORSE RIDING
Relais de Bravone, tel. 95388119
Randonées Equestres de Bravone, tel. 95388064

Calacuccia

Calacuccia is the 'capital' of the fertile Golo valley which used to
grow chestnuts in abundance and sufficient food for each
flock-owning family. The 20th century has brought many changes
to the area: flocks are smaller, shepherds fewer, and ewes' milk
now goes abroad to make Roquefort cheese instead of being

44

processed in the cellars under each neat stone house. Farming, like forestry, has become more organised, while in the 1960s a massive dam, part of a hydroelectric scheme and reservoir system, created a large peaceful lake south of Calacuccia; the Niolo, as well as being a paradise for campers, climbers and walkers, could become a summer lakeside playground. During the winter season there is a small skiing base near the Col de Vergio.

The area remains strong in Corsican crafts and traditions; the three-day Fête de la Santa, each September, when the statue of the Virgin is carried in procession from the church at Calacuccia, keeps alive the chanting songs of the shepherds and the snail-patterned spiral dance called the Granitola.

HOTELS
Les Touristes, tel. 95480004
La Scala, tel. 954480276

Calcatoggio

Near Calcatoggio, at the mouth of the river Liscia, a small development straggles along a nondescript beach, but there are several simple though pleasant hotels and good camping facilities.

USEFUL ADDRESSES

HOTELS
Cinarca, tel. 95213023
Club San Bastiano, tel. 95282035
Castel d'Orcino, tel. 95282063
Monte Narval, tel. 95282535

CAMPING
U Summalu, tel. 95522421
Le Liamone, tel. 95522024
La Liscia, tel. 95522065
Tiuccia, tel. 9552296

Calenzana

The tightly-packed houses of Calenzana, situated about 13 km inland from the resort of Calvi, are dwarfed by a towering 19th century Baroque campanile, in turn overshadowed by the craggy hill at whose foot it stands, and like so many Corsican villages it is almost encircled by two fast-running streams, the Secco and the Bartasca.

The campanile stands on its own, in the centre of a cemetery known as the Campu Santu dei Tedeschi, resting place of German victims of the 1731 campaign when the Genoese enlisted the help of the Emperor Charles VI, during the course of which the village was the scene of a bloody encounter.

The church itself is an 18th century building, erected on the site of the original Romanesque construction and with a plain interior containing no striking paintings to catch the eye. However, only a kilometre further on, in a typical setting of olive groves, is the little white Church of Saint Restitute, dedicated to a Corsican martyr beheaded in 303. Two processions in the saint's honour are held each year: the first takes the statue and the saint's relics to the Église St-Blaise in Calenzana, and the second returns them to Saint Restitute.

Restitute's white marble sarcophagus was discovered by excavators working on the site, which has been identified as that of a Roman necorpolis. The statue of the saint is to be found in the chapel on the left.

Also of interest to the visitor is the Place de l'Hôtel-de-Ville, a large, rectangular square, ornamented with palms.

Nearby
The villages of Zilia, Montemaggiore (with the curious church of St-Rainier), Muro, Speloncato, Belgodre, and the holiday resort of Lozari.

USEFUL ADDRESSES

HOTELS
Monte Grosso, tel. 95627015
Bel Horizon, 4 Place Prince-Pierre, tel. 95627172

CAMPING
Clos du Mouflon, tel. 95650353
Paradella, tel. 95650097

HORSE RIDING
Paglia Orba

BANK
Crédit Agricole, tel. 95627322

CALVI

Calvi, an old citadel town set on a headland in the north of Corsica overlooking a beautiful curve of sandy beach bordered by umbrella pines, is one of the island's biggest, most sophisticated and most attractive holiday resorts.

Popular for many years with discerning holidaymakers, it has several extremely pleasant hotels, a huge selection of friendly restaurants and bars, a casual, easy going attitude to life, and is an ideal base for exploring the north of Corsica, with a variety of delightful, isolated beaches dotted along the coastline.

Restaurants and cafés, vantage points for watching the comings and goings of yachts and fishing boats, keep up a brisk trade until late at night, while the citadel, between the bays of Calvi and Revellata, symbolises almost five centuries of Genoese occupation, and provides excellent sea views from its ramparts.

The long safe sandy beach east of the town shelves gently, is well supplied with cafés and watersports, and looks past the harbour to the mighty citadel on its jutting promontory.

The newer part of the town stretches along the busy port. Quai Landry is palm-lined and attractive, much congested with traffic and animated, especially at night, with open-air restaurants and cafés, while the streets behind hold all the requirements of a modern resort.

Among the red roofs and creamy-grey façades rises the Baroque tower of the lower town's plain white church, begun in 1774 but not completed until 1938. Below the Hôtel de Ville are vivid terraced gardens of palms and flowering shrubs. The citadel, on its high rock, dominates all and massive walls of ochre granite blocks slope up to the tall clustered buildings of the enclosed old town, which is another world of ancient grey houses and twisting, cobbled streets.

PLACES OF INTEREST

Église St Jean-Baptiste
The church's octagonal cupola rises above the justle of red-tiled roofs and its austere white façade dominates the sloping Place d'Armes and the old town. The airy interior of the church, built in the 13th century and reconstructed in the 16th, contains various treasures, notably an ebony Christ and a robed Spanish Virgin, both of which are carried in festival processions. Also of interest are the 16th century baptismal fonts.

Oratoire St-Antoine
An elegant 15th century chapel overlooking the bay, and a storehouse of religious objects and works of art from the 16th to 19th centuries.

Nearby
Beyond the Calvi Ste Catherine airport the road enters the Calenzana Forest, ending at the Auberge de la Forêt, where the porphyry walls of the natural amphitheatre of Bonifato rise above the treelines.

EXCURSIONS
Calvi is well placed for short excursions. By boat the Grotto of the Veaux Marins can be visited in half a day, while the day excursion to Porto via the Golfe de Girolata is one of the finest sea excurions available on the island.

Those hiring cars can sightsee in the nearby mountains or visit the attractive resort of Ile-Rousse; or, alternatively, go further inland into the Balagne region or on to the rugged and dramatic scenery of Cap Corse.

USEFUL ADDRESSES

TOURIST INFORMATION
Chemin de la Plage, tel. 95650587

TRAVEL AGENCIES
Ollandini, 6 Av de la République, tel. 95650674
Calvi Corse Touristique, 4 rue Joffe, tel. 95651135
Les Beaux Voyages, le Vieux Chalet, tel. 95650826

Corse Voyages, Blvd Wilson, tel. 95650047
Sogedis Voyages, Port de Calvi, tel. 95651084
Société Tramcar, Quai Landry, tel. 95651777

CAR HIRE
Agence Les Beaux Voyages, 4 rue Joffre, tel. 95651135
Inter Rent, Quartier Neuf, tel. 95650213
Astolfi, Place de la Porteuse d'eau, tel. 95650173
Avis, Av de la République, tel. 95650674
Citer, airport, tel. 95652339
Europcar, airport, tel. 95652339
Hertz, 2 rue du Maréchal Joffre, tel. 95650664; airport,
    tel. 95650298

BICYCLE HIRE
Balagne Cycles, Av de la République, on the way out of town

HOSPITAL
Antenne Médicale, S.M.U.R. ancient Presbytère, tel. 95651122

HOTELS
Grand, tel. 95650974. (A smart, stylish hotel in the town centre,
    with spacious and elegant bedrooms)
Les Aloes, Quartier Donateo, tel. 95650146
Balanea, 6 rue Clemenceau, tel. 95650045 (a pleasant, three-star
    hotel, many of whose bedrooms overlook the pretty port)
L'Abbaye, rte de Santore, tel. 95650427 (a former Franciscan
    abbey)
Saint-Erasme, rte d'Ajaccio, tel. 95650450
Kalliste, 1 Av Cdt-Marché, tel. 95650981
Le Magnolia, rue Alsace Lorraine, tel. 95651916

CAMPING
Campo di Fiori, tel. 95650243
Dolce Vita, tel. 95650599
La Clé des Champs, tel. 95650086
Paduella, tel. 95650616
Libeccio, tel. 95650150
Bella Vista, tel. 95651176
La Pinede, tel. 95651780
Marinella, tel. 95651704
International, tel. 95650175

HOLIDAY VILLAGES
Club de l'Horizon, tel. 95650058
Club Olympique, tel.95650060
Club Alpin Autrichien, tel. 95650224

RESTAURANTS
La Poème, (located within the walls of the citadel)
Le Royal, 15 rue Clemenceau
Ile de Beauté, Quai Landry, tel. 650046 (one of Corsica's best
    restaurants, specialising in seafood)
Comme chez Soi, Quai Landry, tel. 650059

CABARETS
A Stella, Chez Maryse Nicolai, rue Clemenceau 11, tel. 95650629
Le Byblos, chemin de Santore, tel. 95652250

BOAT HIRE
Calvi Bateau, Quai Landry, tel. 95650291

SKIN DIVING
G.E.T.S., tel.95650011

RAIL STATION
Tel. 95650061

FERRIES
Corsica Ferries, next to the SNCM booth on Quai de Commerce,
    tel. 95651084, sail for Savona in Italy

TENNIS
Tennis Municipaux, tel. 95651429

MINI GOLF
Road to Bastia

HORSE RIDING
Centre Equestre de la Balagne, tel. 95607219

BANKS
Banque Populaire Provençale et Corse, Blvd Wilson,
    tel. 95650887
Crédit Agricole, rue de la République, tel. 95650940

Crédit Lyonnais, Blvd Wilson, tel. 95650827
Société Générale, Blvd Wilson, tel. 95650538

CHEMISTS
Pharmacie de la Serra, Immeuble Laniella, Quartier Santore,
    tel. 95651553
Pharmacie Centrale, Blvd Wilson, tel. 95650854
Pharmacie de la Plage, rue Joffre, tel. 95650024

Campomoro

Located on the Golfe de Valinco, and boasting a Genoese tower
sited at the tip of a small promontory, the tiny port of Campomoro
is attractively situated with a lovely beach and, on its edge, a small
eucalyptus wood.

   Until quite recently it was a charming, unsophisticated seaside
village with a few shops, cottages and villas, but the developers
have since moved in, transforming the village into an attractive
small resort. From the jetty one can look due northwards across
the bay to another small developing holiday resort, Porto Pollo,
which occupies an almost identical position at the tip of a
promontory.

USEFUL ADDRESSES

CAMPING
Lecci e Murta, tel. 95760267
La Vallée, tel. 95742120

CAP CORSE

Cap Corse is the northern extremity of the 40 km chain of mountains forming the spine of Corsica. In this harsh setting maquis has reclaimed the hillsides where once fruit trees, vines and olives grew, and abandoned villages and feudal ruins look like outcrops of the mountains. The sea views are outstanding, especially on the west coast where the cliff road runs high above the saw-tooth coastline. Cape Corse natives, unlike other Corsicans, have always been drawn to the sea and distant lands, such as South America and the West Indies, and imposing houses attest to the profitability of these foreign sojourns.

Characteristic of the peninsula are the marinas, once village extensions for fishing and trading, now given over to tourism. Among the most important of these are Maccinaggio, long a port, now an important marina; and Centuri, with arguably the prettiest and certainly the most unusual marina on the peninsula.

The road around the cape passes sheltered coves and high, forest-covered mountains. Sprinkled amid these hills of chestnut trees, lime trees and olive groves are old fortified towns such as Cagnano, 5½ km inland from the port of Porticciolo, built in the period of Genoese rule, while on the coast you can see the restored Tour de Losse, part of an elaborate system of Genoese towers that could once warn every Corsican within two hours of an impending attack by Barbarians or pirates.

Despite the cool colours of the buildings, the north of the island is hot, and the climate produces good vines, olives and the Corsican version of the lemon called the cedrat, while the peninsula is ringed with Genoese watchtowers and old villages. Even before tourism turned each marina into a budding resort the inhabitants of Cap Corse took more interest in the sea than was habitual in the rest of the island; rather than shepherds they were historically fishermen, sailors and traders. Their ports still thrive, while the villages up in the interior are inevitably becoming depopulated.

Almost every village seems to have its watchtower. That at Nonza is proudly perched on a vertiginous black rock, and lichen-grey houses cluster at the edge of the cliff round the central square and the Eglise-Ste-Julie. Down many zig-zagging steps is Ste-Julie's marble shrine and 'fountain.'

Cargèse

The pretty, red-roofed village of Cargèse lies at the northern end of the Golfe de Sagone, its houses rising in tiers on the steep hillside, with a tiny port lying far below at the foot of a hill. Formerly a Greek colony for refugees from Turkish persecution, Cargèse still has a Greek orthodox church, which stares sombrely across at its Roman Catholic counterpart on the other side of the valley. Both churches share one thing in common, in that they shelter attractive images of Saint John the Baptist. That in the orthodox church is a typical Byzantine icon, the saint's features being sharp with a clarity of line; that in the Roman Catholic church forms part of a group with the Virgin Mary, Saint Elizabeth and the child Christ, the creation of an anonymous artist.

On the headland is another of the innumerable Genoese watchtowers which are such a feature of the landscape.

There are several sandy beaches near Cargèse; just outside the town is the Plage di Chiuni, guarded by the Genoese tower, and offering a large beach of white sand together with a holiday village; to the south is the Plage de Rocca Marina, which occupies a bay protected by the points of Cargèse and of Molendino; and also to the south is the Plage de Menasina, another lovely beach of fine white sand.

The coast bordering Cargèse offers several small hotels, some self-catering apartments, camping sites and a Club Med. village. These resorts are good for very peaceful beach holidays, but there is little to do except sunbathing on the beach, so a car is useful.

USEFUL ADDRESSES

TOURIST INFORMATION
Rue du Docteur Dragacci, tel. 95264131

HOTELS
Les Lentisques, rte du Pero. tel. 95264234
Helios, tel. 95264124
Beau Rivage, tel. 95264391
La Spelunca, tel. 95264012

CAMPING
Torracci, tel. 95264239

RESTAURANT
A Volta, Place du Chamoine Mattei, tel. 95264196

CAR RENTAL
Station Elf, tel. 95264109

CENTURI-PORT

With its highly picturesque, green-tile roofed houses, miniature harbour, and small sandy beach, the village of Centuri-Port is both delightful and relatively unspoilt – and its restaurant serve arguably the best langouste on the island, though they are not cheap. Hotels in the port tend to be simple and unsophisticated, but how long this will remain so is a matter for speculation, since Centuri is being 'discovered', and pleasure boats now share the picture-postcard harbour with the lobster fishers, who present a colourful scene bringing in their daily catch.

USEFUL ADDRESSES

HOTELS
Du Vieux Moulin, tel. 95356015 (only one star, but a delightful,
    old-fashioned hotel right by the fishing harbour)
Du Pêcheur, tel. 95356014
Centuri, tel. 95356170

CAMPING
L'Isoluttu, tel. 95356281

RESTAURANTS
Le Pêcheur, tel. 95356014
Le Vieux Moulin, tel. 95356015
Le Centuri, tel. 95356170
La Jetée, tel. 95356008

Cervione

The village of Cervione boasts two buildings of considerable
interest: an imposing cathedral built at the end of the 16th century
for Saint Alexandre Sauli who was canonised in 1904, and which
contains remarkable 17th century choir stalls; and, just outside the
village, the little Romanesque chapel of Ste-Christine containing
some interesting frescoes. There is also a small museum here
depicting the history, archaeology, ethnology and religious art of
the region.

USEFUL ADDRESSES

HOTEL
Saint-Alexandre, tel. 95381083

CAMPING
Campoloro, tel. 95380020

BANK
Crédit Agricole, tel. 95380370

Monte Cinto

The highest peak in the island, at 2,700 metres, Monte Cinto is
eternally covered by snow, even though it is only 25 km from the
sea. The ascent in summer is not technically difficult, providing you
are fit, the weather is good, and you are prepared to make a dawn
start. The best approach is by the south-east face from Calacuccia,
from where you can drive by road to within 6 km of the summit.
After that it is hard going, but depending on your fitness you
should reach the top in 4–5 hours. From the summit there are truly
breathtaking views of the whole island, and across the seas to the
Alpes-Maritimes, Italy and Elba.

Corbara

The little village of Corbara, which overlooks the major holiday resort of Ile-Rousse, is sprawled over the slopes of Mont de Guido, and dominated by the ruins of a castle, family home of the Savellis who claim descent from a Roman prince who emigrated from the mainland in the 9th century. Establishing themselves as one of the great families of the Balagne, the Savellis assumed the title of Count of Balagne after being the architects of numerous victories over the Saracens.

Not far from the village is the Convent of Corbara, built in 1430 at the foot of Monte Sant'Angelo by Mgr Nicolas Savelli, and transformed into a convent in 1456. The monastery was ruined during the Revolution, the peaceful Franciscans being driven out in 1792, victims of revolutionary cant, but in 1857 the semi-ruin was taken over by the Dominicans who reconstructed and extended it, and turned it into a philosophical and theological college.

USEFUL ADDRESSES

CAMPING
Le Bodri, tel. 95601086

CORTE

Corte, the largest Corsican town not on the coast, is a pleasant town and a symbol of independence in the heart of the island: from 1755 to 1769 it was Paoli's capital, and as the seat of Corsica university embodies the island's cultural identity.

The town is situated on the summit and flank of a massive crag near the confluences of the Tavignano, Restonica and Orta rivers, and is protected by water on three sides while the citadel surmounts an impregnable crag with a vast panorama of the surrounding valleys. The town's situation as the focus of natural routeways also stamps it as the virtual crossroads of the island, for it commands the central furrow aligned north and south at the point where it intersects with the only practicable east-west route from Bastia to Ajaccio. To the north-east the Golo Valley gives access to Bastia, and north-westwards, via the Col de Vizzavona, to the Balagne and Calvi; to the south-east, the Tavignano valley skirts the Castagniccia to reach the Plain of Aleiria.

Corte is traditional Corsica, the Corsica of the 'patriots' and the heroes – Vincentello d'Istria, Sampiero and Pascal Paoli. In direct contrast with Calvi and Bonifacio, it was a city the Genoese could never hold, let alone subdue.

Apart from the citadel, the old town buildings are characterless and of little architectural significance, while the lower town is being victimised by the construction of standard blocks of offices and flats in disharmony with the surroundings.

Yet the town does have atmosphere, and even without pre-knowledge of history, one can sense its violent past, the fact that the narrow streets, dark unfriendly frontages, and silent stone stairways, have been the scenes or murder, battle, treachery, triumph and despair.

The Légionnaires inhabit the old citadel of Vincentello, hanging

59

like an eagle's nest on its crag above the Tavignano river and here, as in Calvi, their originally dreaded arrival has been a boon to local tradesmen, and provided husbands for a number of local girls.

On the Place Paoli is the house where Madame Mère gave birth to the eldest of her five sons, Joseph, later King of Spain, and which was the family home of one of Napoléon's most talented leaders, Arrighi de Casanove, later Duke of Padua and Governor of Corsica during the Hundred Days.

The centre of Corte is the Place Gaffori, named after Général Gaffori (1704–1753), and the house where the general was born, situated opposite the church of the Annunciation, displays a bullet-pitted wall, reminding one of the moment when the indomitable Madame Faustine Gaffori, besieged by the Genoese, threatened to blow up her house and everybody in it if the word surrender was ever breathed.

Apart from a statue on the Place Paoli, unveiled in 1854, Pascal Paoli's memory is perpetuated by the Palais National, now a museum and library. In Paoli's day the building, more a large provincial residence than a palace, housed not only the experimental Corsican Parliament brought into existence by Paoli's Constitution, but also professors and a sprinkling of the students of the all-Corsican University Paoli had opened in 1765.

PLACES OF INTEREST

National Palace (seat of the independent government of Corsica), citadel and belvedere overlooking the Tavignano and Restonica gorges.

EXCURSIONS
The Restonica Gorge (15 km south-west) is the starting point for several interesting hikes, such as to lakes Melo and Capitello. The scenery is magnificent: a crystal-clear trout-stream, its banks lined with fig, poplar and chestnut trees, cascades down the mountain sides.
Sermano   One of the rare villages where Mass is still sung in the old Corsican settings for male voices.

USEFUL ADDRESSES

TOURIST INFORMATION
Hôtel de la Paix, tel. 95460672

HOTELS
Sampiero Corso, Av du Patg-Pierucci, tel. 95460976
La Paix, tel. 95460672
Auberge de la Restonica, at the entrance to the Restonica Gorge,
    tel. 95460958

CAMPING
Camping de Tuani, tel. 95461165
Les Cascades, tel. 95369191
L'Alivettu, tel. 95461109
Sognu, Faubourg Scaravaglie, tel. 95460907

RESTAURANTS
Chez Julien, Cours Paoli 24, tel. 95460290
La Restonica, rte de la Restonica, tel. 95460958

TRAVEL AGENCY
Ollandini, Place Xavier-Lucciani, tel. 95462554

CAR HIRE
Citer, Garage du Tavignanu, tel. 95461728
Pietrantoni, 19 Cours Paoli, tel. 95461277
Solvet, Av de la Poretta, tel. 95460203

HOSPITAL
Hôpital Civil, La Gare, tel. 95460136

BANKS
Caisse d'Epargne P.T.T., tel. 95460820
Crédit Agricole, Cours Paoli 19, tel. 95460975
Crédit Lyonnais, Cours Paoli 17, tel. 95460063
Société Générale, Cours Paoli 24, tel. 95460081

HORSE RIDING
Corsica Ranch, Vertanesa

Desert Des Agriates

Although much of Corsica is made up of trees, meadows, orchards
and bright waters, the island also contains an area of 40,000 acres

that is totally uncultivated and uninhabited – the Desert des Agriates. It is stony, rocky waste land, grey and mournful, coming to life only in spring when the 'fire' anemones flower. It is one of the few places in Europe where summer heat attains an almost Saharan intensity.

Evisa

It would be difficult to find a more attractive site in Corsica than that of Evisa, a village situated 2,723 feet above sea level. It stands near some of the most striking scenery in Corsica, with the gorges of Spelunca, the forest of Aitone and the Vergio Pass all being noteworthy, making it an ideal base for those who enjoy walking. Sloping steeply like the typical fortress village, its houses cluster tightly on the spur separating the Porto River valley and the narrow ravine of the Aitone torrent.

USEFUL ADDRESSES

HOTELS
U'Castellu, tel. 262071
Aitone, tel. 95262004
Scopa Rossa, tel. 262002

HOLIDAY VILLAGE
Paesolu d'Aitone, tel. 95262039

CAMPING
L'Acciola, tel. 95262301

Filitosa

Important discoveries have been made in the neighbourhood of the village of Filitosa, located 18 km from the west coast resort of Propriano. Here all three stages of prehistoric civilisation are presented: the simple dolmens and standing stones, the more elaborate sculptured menhirs, and the complete camps of the Torreen culture.

Filitosa lies in the shallow valley of the Tarova close by a narrow road that branches off the main road a few kilometres above Olmeto, and is easily located and well sign-posted. The site has been progressively opened up for more than two decades, and reveals Filitosa's intermixture of three prehistoric cultures, all megalithic, with the earliest dating back at least five thousand years. The first inhabitants of this low-lying west-corner of the island were the race now believed responsible for many standing-stones and stone-alignments such as those at Renaggiu, Stantari and Pallagiu.

The site also contains an enormous menhir, lying full-length on the ground, together with a selection of other menhir figures carved from blocks of granite.

PLACES OF INTEREST

Museum displays excavated artefacts.
Oppidium a group of fortifications and religious monuments fashioned from large boulders. The remains of a Torreen village and five menhirs in a quarry are still visible.

Galeria

Overlooked, like so many Corsican villages, by the remains of a Genoese tower, Galéria lies on the left bank of the River Fango, on a charming open bay, and though limited development has taken place over recent years it remains a charming small seaside resort, best suited to those looking for a peaceful and relaxing holiday.

USEFUL ADDRESSES

HOTELS
Du Fango, tel. 95620192
Filosorma, tel. 95620002
Auberge de la Ferrayola, tel. 95620152

CAMPING
Ideal Camping, tel. 95620146
Les 2 Torrens, tel. 95620067

HORSE RIDING
Cavalli di Filosorma, tel. 95620025

Ghisonaccia

Ghisonaccia, built by the mouth of the Fium Orbo (the blind) river, is a prosperous and attractive village on the edge of lovely scenery, with roads plunging through narrow gorges. Of interest in the neighbourhood are the vast lagoon of Urbino, to the north, where mussels and oysters are bred, and the vast beaches of Pinia and Vignale. At nearby Poggio di Nazza are many delightful old houses, while 27 km away is the pleasant village of Ghisoni.

USEFUL ADDRESSES

TOURIST INFORMATION
Mairie, tel. 95561510/560121

HOTEL
Motel Sud, tel. 95560054

CAMPING
Arinella Bianca, tel. 95560478
Marine de Caprone, tel. 95564202

HORSE RIDING
'Cavallu di Fium'Orbu,' tel. 95562322
Centre d'Equitation de Calzarello, tel. 95560745

BANKS
Caisse d'Epargne P.T.T., tel. 95560100
Banque Worms, tel. 95560909
Crédit Lyonnais, route de la Gare, tel. 95560136
Société Générale, immeubale Fiumorbo, tel. 95561518

CAR HIRE
Citer, tel. 95560981

Ghisoni

Tucked away at the head of a valley, hemmed in by trees and
completely shadowed by two mountains curiously named Kyrie
Elaison and Christe Elaison, Ghisoni is a pleasant village with a
handsome church, and is a good base for exploring the woodland
scenery in the neighbourhood, and for a longer excursion to Monte
Renoso, offering tremendous views. At 2,352 metres, Monte
Renoso is one of the five highest peaks in Corsica, and appears like
a massive dome. From the summit there is a glorious panorama of
the whole of the south of the island, of the gulfs of Valinco and
Ajaccio, and also of the island of Sardinia.
    Other interesting excursions are through the forests of Ghisoni
and Marmano.

USEFUL ADDRESS

HOTEL
Kyrie, tel. 95576033

Guagno-Les-Bains

A new thermal baths has been constructed here in the valley of the
Fiume Grosso in an effort to reintroduce the idea of health resorts
into the Corsican hospitality scene. The waters of Guagno were
being used for this purpose as long ago as the 16th century –
although it was not until the 18th century that their properties were
fully realised – and many famous Corsicans have tried them out
over the years, including Pascal Paoli, Letizia Bonaparte, and
Napoléon himself, accompanied by his brother Joseph.

EXCURSIONS
Interesting excursions can be made from here to Orto, which

occupies an impressive site at the bottom of the valley; and the village of Soccia, perched on the hillside. Soccia is also the point of departure for excusions to Creno lake.

ILE-ROUSSE

Situated to the east of Calvi, and one of Corsica's oldest holiday resorts, Ile-Rousse was founded in 1769 by Pascal Paoli. It gets its name (Red Island) from the red-ochre islet of Pietra which boasts a lighthouse, is connected to the shore by a jetty, and which contrasts with the sparkling blue waters and maquis-covered hills.
Ile-Rousse is a relaxing town with shaded squares reminiscent of France, pavement cafés and restaurants, many keenly contested games of 'boules', and an attractive little promenade opened in 1984.

The beaches on both sides of the resort are clean and sandy and there is a good variety of watersports, such as windsurfing, sailing, snorkelling, water-skiing and diving, complemented by a few beach bars. The town itself contains a good selection of restaurants, cafés and some local nightlife, although on the whole Ile-Rousse is more geared towards the slightly older age group.

Place Paoli is a lovely rectangular square, bordered by cafés, and extremely animated. Near the centre four tall palm trees surround a fountain surmounted on a bust of Pascal Paoli.

The old town, to the north of Place Paoli, includes a covered market containing boutiques and shops, while at the entrance to rue Notre-Dame, facing Place Tino-Rossi, is a half-ruined tower carrying an inscription commemorating the founding of the town. Behind the square is an esplanade with a monument to the dead, sculptured by Volti.

A train covers the coast between Calvi and Ile-Rousse, with frequent departures during the high season. The line is divided into three sections, and one can save money by buying a carnet of six tickets. Another train links Ile-Rousse with Bastia, a journey of about two and a half hours.

EXCURSIONS

Ile-Rousse is a good base for various interesting excursions, notably to Monticello, a pleasant village surrounded by olive trees and boasting a huge square bordered by ancient houses; and to the Baroque church of Santa Reparata-di-Balagne, whose terrace offers a view of Ile-Rousse to the north, the valley of Regino to the north-east, and the mountain chain of Monte Grosso to the south; and finally to the village of Corbara.

USEFUL ADDRESSES

TOURIST INFORMATION
Rue J. Galizi, tel. 95600435

HOTELS
Napoléon Bonaparte, Place Paoli, tel. 95600609 (in the grand
    manner, and well located)
La Pietra, rte du Port, tel. 95600145
Isola Rossa, tel. 95600132

DISCOTHEQUES
I Certalli, Blvd de Fogata, tel. 95600505
Challenger, Av Calizzi, tel. 95602089

TRAVEL AGENCY
Mariani, Place Paoli, tel. 95601129

CAR HIRE
Avis, 3 rue Général Graziani, tel. 95601191
Citer, Place Paoli, tel. 956011119
Europcar, 3 Place Paoli, tel. 95600830

BOAT HIRE
Balagne Sport, rue Napoléon, tel. 95600517

HORSE RIDING
Ranch 'Cantarettu-City,' route d'Algajola, tel. 95607089 or
    95600862

SKIN DIVING
Poséidon Nemrod Club, Plage de l'Ile-Rousse, tel. 95651122

BANKS
Caisse d'Epargne P.T.T., tel. 95600197
Banque Populaire Provençale et Corse, tel. 956000058
Crédit Agricole, Av Piccioni, tel. 9500182
Crédit Lyonnais, Place Paoli, tel. 956000280
Société Geńérale, Av Piccioni, tel. 95600474

Lozari

The small holiday resort of Lozari lies to the east of Ile-Rousse
among a group of sandy beaches in a peaceful area, and is the last
of Corsica's western coast resorts: the island's north-west corner is
the arid, empty Desert des Agriates. Facilities are limited in
comparison with the larger, more developed resorts, and
consequently the beaches tend to be much quieter.

USEFUL ADDRESS

CAMPING
Annabel, tel. 95601421

Macinaggio

The village of Macinaggio, once part of a rich but more recently
depressed area, is in the process of being converted into a modern
holiday resort, of particular interest to yachtsmen, with a newly
expanded pleasure port. The climate here is relatively mild and,
unlike the rather austere grandeur of much of the island, the
scenery in the immediate surroundings is relaxing and gentle.
　　The village was the scene of Pasal Paoli's disembarkation on his
native soil in 1790 after 21 years of exile, spent mostly in London,
Napoléon stayed here, too, after his flight from Ajaccio in 1793,
and prior to his abortive attempt to persuade Bastia to renounce
Paoli and remain faithful to France. Of interest is the Romanesque
chapel of Santa Maria.

EXCURSIONS

From Macinaggio a fascinating excursion can be made to one of the most impressive mountain villages in the whole of Corsica: Rogliano. It clings defiantly to the mountain slopes, and boasts a huge number of ancient dwellings, three castles, the colossal church of St-Angel, and fortified towers clinging to the rock. It was once a powerful stronghold that controlled the north of Cap Corse.

USEFUL ADDRESSES

HOTELS
Bellini, tel. 95354305
Les Iles, tel. 95354302

CAMPING
De la Plage, tel. 95354376

HORSE RIDING
Haras di i Gioielli, tel. 95354274

BOAT HIRE
Cap Corse Voile, Port de Plaisance, tel. 95354147

Montemaggiore

The birthplace of Don Juan's mother, Montemaggiore is a delightful village perched on cliffs, and splendid panoramas can be enjoyed from its central square embracing the Secco valley with its ocean of olive trees, Calvi's distant ramparts, and the Mediterranean. Also of interest is Montemaggiore's delicate Baroque church.

Just outside the village is the Chapelle St-Rainier in Romanesque-Pisan style, whose interior contains interesting windows decorated with curious, grimacing images.

Moriani Plage

A dusty little town with a long sandy beach, Moriani Plage is attracting tourist development, although it lacks the scenic appeal of many other Corsican resorts.

USEFUL ADDRESSES

TOURIST INFORMATION
Mairie, tel. 95385087

HOTELS
San Lucianu, tel. 95385175
Alba Serena, tel. 95385789
Corsica, tel. 95385005
La Monte Cristo, tel. 95315682

HOLIDAY VILLAGE
Résidence Soliciana, tel. 95385015

BANKS
Crédit Agricole, tel. 95385025
Crédit Lyonnais, tel. 95385164

Morosaglia

A small town set in the green heart of the Castigniccia, a region of chestnut forests, Morosaglia is a collection of hamlets, among them Stretta, where Pascal Paoli, 'father' of the Corsican nation, was born in a house which is now a museum. It is a pleasant little museum, full of personal souvenirs, including a collection of proclamations printed by the Press Paoli himself founded during the days when Corsica belonged to the Corsicans. On the walls are engravings of the portraits of the Babbu della Patria, one of the most popular subjects for portrait painters of the era. Although originally buried in London, Paoli's remains were brought back to the island in 1889 and now rest in a chapel in what was the ground floor of the house.

Morosaglia is also the resting place of Pascal's elder brother Clemente, buried in what is now a school endowed in the terms of his will, while a short walk up the hill is the old parish church of Santa Reparata where Pascal was baptized.

USEFUL ADDRESS

HOTEL
Des Touristes, tel. 95476070 (tiny and very simple)

Nebbio

The Nebbio is the region behind the Golfe de St-Florent, a landscape of fertile hills and valleys encircled by mountains. Like the Balagne, the areas has vineyards, orchards, meadows and picturesque villages, while characteristic of the region are the houses built of thick brownish stone slabs which are also used for the dry-stone walls. Among the most attractively set of the villages are Oletta and San-Pietro-di-Tenda. Of the many interesting churches that of Murato is outstanding: a remarkable mixture of Pisan Romanesque and more Barbaric decorative elements, its simple rectangle having a tall western bell tower half supported on fat round columns of alternating white and green slabs. Around windows and blind arches, and in less likely places, there is a mass of astonishing carving – symbolic beasts, enigmatic figures and Biblical themes.

Nonza

The village of Nonza is nothing less than astonishing, perched on a dark rock, crowned by a fortified tower, and with houses seeming to sprout from the cliffs which serve as their foundation. It was here that a young Christian was tortured for refusing to abjure her faith, and legend has it that little springs at the foot of the cliffs gushed miraculously as the girl's servered breasts fell on the rocks.

Today, twin jets of water represent the two 'miraculous' springs. The dark grey beach beyond the town is vast, and generally practically deserted.

USEFUL ADDRESSES

HOTELS
Auberge Patrizi, tel. 95378216

RESTAURANTS
Pizzeria 'A Stalla', tel. 95378372
Creperie 'U Franghju', tel. 95378469

Piana

This is one of the most delightful coastal villages in Corsica, with sheer, jutting cliffs of rose-coloured granite, fragrant eucalyptus trees and sandy beaches. In summer it is a very lively spot, and presents an harmonious and attractive picture.

Located on a plateau 438 metres above sea level, and facing the isles of Sennino and Scandola, Piana is dominated by a beautiful white church topped by a bell-tower mounted on a dome in the form of a lantern. Built in the Italian style at the end of the 18th century, the church is dedicated to Sainte Marie.

The village retains a typically Corsican character. At its southern extremity is Firajola creek, with red rocks tumbling into the sea, rich in langoustes, and beyond the nearby hamlet of Vistale is the magnificent white sandy beach of Arone.

Nearby, the Calanche de Piana offers spectacular scenery with huge red mountains plunging into little bays filled with emerald and black water. If you are here early in the morning you might catch a glimpse of the rare African fish-eagle, since this area is its only known European habitat.

USEFUL ADDRESSES

HOTELS
Capo Rossa, tel. 95261235

L'Horizon, tel. 295268007
Les Calanches, tel. 95261208
Hôtel Mare e Monti, tel. 95268214 (the newest hotel in the region, a small, 15-room establishment well-equipped and with good views)

Pino

Pino, located on Cap Corse, is a charming village distinguished by its excellent site among vines and olives, fruit and flowers, and boasting numerous ancient houses, Genoese towers, a church and many funerary chapels surrounded by cypress trees.

The church of Ste-Marie, which faces the sea, was restored in the 18th and 19th centuries and presents a lovely Baroque-style façade. The ancient convent of St-Francis is located on the little road descending to the tiny marina of Pino, and stands next to an old Genoese tower. The interior of the chapel contains some interesting frescoes.

5 km away, on the Col Ste-Lucie, is the Torre di Seneca, said to have been the philosophers' prison in the years AD 43–49.

USEFUL ADDRESS

HOTEL
Alard, tel. 95350176

PORTICCIO

Porticcio is a bright little modern, purpose-built beach resort on one of the sandy coves of the Gulf of Ajaccio, and commands a stunning view of a great curve of blue water with a backdrop of mountain slopes. The beach itself is of coarse sand but is wide and attractive, and well equipped with beach bars and restaurants. At one end of the little bay is a pleasing development of bars and shops, including a small cinema and car rental companies. Public transport is poor, but you can hire a car for the half hour journey to Ajaccio, which is about 16 km away, or for exploring further up the coast, or inland to spectacular mountain scenery.

USEFUL ADDRESSES

TOURIST INFORMATION, tel. 95250574

HOTELS
Thalassa Sofitel, tel. 95250034 (a luxury, four-star establishment with excellent facilities)
Maquis, tel. 95250555
Isolella, tel. 95254136
Hotel de Casavone, tel. 95250916 (an attractive development of self-catering studios with their own little terraces, located near the ruins of the Capitello tower).

CAMPING
U Prunelli, tel. 95200051
Benista, tel. 95200441
Mare e Macchia, tel. 95251058
Europe, 95254294
Le Sud, tel. 95254051

HOLIDAY VILLAGE
Mare e Macchia, tel. 95251058

RESTAURANT
L'Auberge Corse, Centre Commercial, tel. 95252572 (a good
value restaurant with generous proportions)
Mare e Macchia, tel. 95252058

HORSE RIDING
Centre Equestre de Porticcio, tel. 95250341

TENNIS
Tennis-Club de Porticcio, Terra Bella, tel. 95251277

MINI GOLF
Résidence Marina Viva, tel. 95250315

CABARET
Le Liberty

DISCOTHÈQUES
Discothèque le Galatée, tel. 95251630
Le Blue Moon, tel. 95250770

CINEMA
Les 3 Stars

BANKS
Crédit Agricole, Res. Le Vesco, tel. 95250012
Société Générale, Res. Golfe, tel. 95251180

Porticciolo

A pleasant little resort on the east coast of Corsica, on an attractive
bay of sand and pebbles, Porticciolo is an ideal resort for those
looking for relative peace and quiet. Nearby is another little resort,
Santa Severa, which is also undergoing touristic development,
thanks to its pleasant setting.

USEFUL ADDRESS

HOTEL
Le Caribou, tel. 95350033/95350233

PORTO

Surrounded by salty blue waters, scented by eucalyptus groves, shadowed by pink granite cliffs and bordered by a winding stream, Porto is located on the west of the island and, being a fishing village, one of the highlights is to take a stroll to the small port area to watch the local fishermen, or better still take to the sea oneself for a trip round the beautiful gulf.

A small, modern resort, it is located at the bottom of a steep lane, and its buildings are constructed from a version of the local stone. The street leading down to the port is lined with shops, cafés and hotels, while more hotels and fast-food restaurants cluster round the harbour area.

The beach, divided from the port by a tall rock with a Genoese tower, and approached by an arched footbridge, is shingle and pebbles as opposed to powder sand, but is attractive and offers excellent watersports facilities. There are several pleasant restaurants and cafés in the village centre, although on the whole facilities are surprisingly poor considering that Porto is such a popular resort.

EXCURSIONS
Being situated on the west coast half way between Calvi and Ajaccio, Porto provides an ideal base for exploring the splendid coastal scenery to the north and south as well as inland to the old capital of Corte. A popular excursion is to the beautiful Porto Valley, which offers the remarkable scenery of Spelunca, the Forest of Aitone, and the coast of the Gulf of Porto. Another interesting excursion is to the village of Ota, 5 km away, which is located at the foot of huge red and rosé rocks and contains many picturesque old houses.

From Porto small roads each side of the river run high along the mountainside to meet at the point where the Aitone torrent and its tributary the Lonca form the river Porto. A footpath from the crossroads leads down nearer the rushing waters, which are invisible from the roads.

Also popular are boat trips to the Scandola, the Calanche de Piana, and to Girolata, a little isolated village on a promontory dominated by a Genoese fort, and making a living from fishing and tourism.

USEFUL ADDRESSES

TOURIST INFORMATION
La Marine, tel. 95261055

CAR AND BOAT HIRE
Auto-Location, tel. 95261474 and 95261172

HOTELS
Kalliste, at the marina, tel. 95261030
Flots Bleus, at the marina, tel. 95261126
Capo d'Orto, rte de Calvi, tel. 95261114
Marina, tel. 95261034
Mediterraneé, tel. 95261027
Le Porto, road to Calvi, tel. 95261120

RESTAURANTS
U Pescador, on the beach, tel. 95261519
L'Oasis, also on the beach, tel. 95261053

CAMPING
Les Oliviers, tel. 95261449
Sole e Vista, tel. 95261571

BANKS
Banque Populaire Provençale et Corse, tel. 95261171
Crédit Agricole, tel. 95261415

PORTO POLLO

Porto Pollo is a delightful little, unpretentious resort in a tranquil setting. It has a small, sheltered harbour bordering a long, narrow stretch of sandy beach, with trees and maquis forming an appealing backdrop, and mountain views across the bay.

USEFUL ADDRESSES

HOTELS
Les Eucalyptus, tel. 95740152
Du Golfe, tel. 95740166
L'Escale, tel. 95740113

HOLIDAY VILLAGE
Arena d'Oro, tel. 95740113
Valinco Village, tel. 95740178

CAMPING
U Casello, tel. 95740180

PORTO-VECCHIO

Porto-Vecchio, set deep in the gulf of the same name, is one of Corsica's premier holiday resorts, with much to commend it. Founded by the Greeks, Roman ships took away the local cork as a form of tax, the Genoese built fortifications before succumbing to the local malaria, and for centuries the town was neglected and largely depopulated, so that little of historic interest remains.

Porto-Vecchio has a new lease of life, however, as a major centre of Corsica's tourist trade, rapidly provided with facilities begun in 1965, agreeably planned and still expanding. Streets full of small shops, delightful if expensive restaurants, and travel agencies lead from the small central square with its church and open-air cafés. There are some small hotels in town, but most are a little way outside, making a car virtually essential.

The beach in the town itself is nothing special, but within easy driving distance lie many of the finest beaches in Corsica, among them that of Palombaggia, south of the rocky headland of La Chiappa: in idyllic surroundings, backed by a ridge of pines and dunes, this long beach is split by red rocks into several sheltered shallow coves, and delightfully secluded parts can be reached by walking. Further south lie the sandy beaches of Santa-Giulia, with many villas and a Club Med. complex, and Rondinara beach, peaceful, though difficult to reach.

USEFUL ADDRESSES

TOURIST INFORMATION
2, rue du Maréchal Juin, tel. 95700958

CAR HIRE
Avis, rue Pasteur, tel. 95730128

Citer, Relais Total des Quatre-Chemins, tel. 95701056
Europcar, La Poretta, tel. 95701555
Hertz, tel. 95730247
Maggiore, Garage Auto Sport, tel. 95701506
Maglioli, rue Colonel Quenza, tel. 95700897

BOAT HIRE
Raffin Marine, Magasin sur le port
S.C.I.M. Corse, route de l'Ospédale, tel. 95701673
L'Helice, 20137 Trinitie de Porto-Vecchio, tel. 95702397
Europ Yachting, marina, tel. 95701869
Aeronautic, tel. 95700496

SKIN DIVING
Club 'La Palanquée', 6 rue Napoléon
La Barraquada, Centre Naturiste de la Chiappa Palombaggia

HORSE RIDING
'Stabbiacciu' stables, tel. 95701730
Ranch du Stabiacco, rte de Sotta, tel. 95701730
Ranch'O Club, Cala Rossa, tel. 9570033

TENNIS
Tennis-Raquette Club, La Poretta, tel. 95702310

WINDSURFING
Yacht Club, tel. 95700056

HOSPITAL
Antenne Médicale, A.M.U., tel. 95701752 or 95700018

BANKS
Caisse d'Epargne P.T.T., tel. 95702155
B.I.A.O. 14 rue Maréchal Juin, tel. 95701815
B.N.P., 9 Av Général Leclerc, tel. 95701619
Banque Populaire Provençale et Corse, tel. 95702314
Crédit Agricole (Bonifacio road) tel. 95700583 and 95700190
Crédit Lyonnais, tel. 95700348
Société Générale, immeuble Filippi (Bastia road) tel. 95701015

TRAVEL AGENCIES
Riva Corse, 13 rue du Général de Gaulle, tel. 95701231

Trinitours, rue Pasteur, tel. 95701383
Corsicatours, 7 rue Jean-Jaurès, tel. 95701036
Ollandini, 6 rue Jean-Jaurès, tel. 95701477

HOTELS
Cala Rossa, tel. 95716151
Cala Verde, tel. 95701155
Shegara, tel. 95700431
Marina di Fiori, tel. 95701631
L'Aiglon, rte du Port, tel. 95701306
Roches Blanches, tel. 95700696
Le Goeland, at the marina, tel. 95701415
San Giovanni, rte d'Arca, tel. 95702225 (a small, family-run hotel
   in a peaceful rural position 3 km inland; the main house is
   charmingly decorated with lots of interesting personal touches)

CAMPING
Les Ilots d'Or, tel. 95700130
La Baie des Voiles, tel. 95700123
Les Chênes, tel. 95700985
Cupulatta, tel. 95700911
Golfo di Sogno, tel. 95700898 (an excellently equipped camping
   site)

HOLIDAY VILLAGE
Golfo di Sogno, tel. 95700898

NATURIST VILLAGES
La Chiappa, tel. 95700031 (a huge holiday village with 240
   bungalows and camping places for 220)
U Furu, rte de Muratello, tel. 95703510

RESTAURANTS
La Marine, Quai Paoli, tel. 95700833
Chez Anna, tel. 957011997
La Forstière, Quatre-Chemins, tel. 95701523

TAXIS
Station cours Napoléon, Place de la République, tel. 95700849

POLICE, tel. 95700017

PROPRIANO

A popular summer resort and a busy fishing village, Propriano lies
in a marvellously protected position at the head of the Gulf of
Valinco, and its initial growth was as the marina for Sartène, the
port serving the Taravo valley, Baraci and Rizzanese valleys, and
as a local fishing port. Known to Phoenician, Greek and Etruscan
traders, it dwindled in importance over the centuries, and
remained relatively undisturbed for hundreds of years until being
discovered by tourists in the 1960s, thanks to its setting on the gulf,
the attractions of the old town, the fine beaches and the growth of
yachting and cruising. As a result the village is developing into a
major holiday resort, with long sandy beaches, lovely views of the
sea and mountains, animated beachside cafés, hotels, restaurants,
holiday villas, every type of aquatic sport, and plenty of interest
inland. At the height of the season Propriano practically rivals
Calvi in terms of tourist animation.

EXCURSIONS
Propriano is well situated for an exploration of the shores of the
Gulf of Valinco, one of the largest and most deserted gulfs of the
island. Interesting excursions can also be made to the prehistoric
monuments of Filitosa and the Rizzanese valley, while the historic
town of Sartène is within easy reach.

USEFUL ADRESSES

TOURIST INFORMATION
rue du Général de Gaulle, tel. 95760149

TRAVEL AGENCY
Ollandini, rue du Général de Gaulle, tel. 95760076

CAR HIRE
Avis, rue du Général de Gaulle, tel. 95760076; airport,
   tel. 95760087
CITER, rue du Général de Gaulle, tel. 95760536

BOAT HIRE
Propriano Yachting, Av Napoléon, tel. 95760343
Corse Nautique Valinco, rue du 9 Septembre, tel. 95760352
Corsica Yachting, Port de Plaisance, tel. 95760929

SKIN DIVING
Centre Aquatique de Propriano, Salon de Thé, Av Napoléon

HORSE RIDING
Centre Equestre de Baracci, tel. 95760802
'Ranch,' on the Sartène road

HOTELS
Le Barracci, tel. 95760114
Arena Bianca, tel. 95760601
Roc e Mar, tel. 95760485
Lido, tel. 95760637

HOLIDAY VILLAGE
Le Corsaire, tel. 95760177

CAMPING
Le Colomba, 2 km away on the road to Baracci, tel. 95760642
Corsica, tel. 95760057
Vigna Maggiore, tel. 95760207
Tikiti, tel. 95760832

RESTAURANTS
Chez Parenti, Av Napoléon, tel. 95761214
Le Cabanon, Av de la Marine, tel. 95760776 (terrace by the sea)
U Tavonu, rue Camille-Pietri, tel. 95761110

TENNIS
Parc des Sports, quartier Saint-Joseph, tel. 95761335

MINI-GOLF
Hôtel Ollandini, tel. 95760510

TAXIS
Station, 1 Av Napoléon, tel. 95760458

BANKS
Banque Worms, Av Napoléon, tel. 95760630
Banque Populaire Provençale, rue du 9 Septembre, tel. 95760463
Crédit Agricole, 21 rue du 9 Septembre, tel. 95760413
Crédit Lyonnais, Av Napoléon, tel. 95760336
Société Générale, rue Camille Pietri, tel. 95760544

Sagone

A friendly little seaside village where the emphasis is on
watersports and the outdoor life, Sagone is very popular with
British holidaymakers, attracted by its wide bay and sandy beach,
and the fact that it is a good place to perfect the art of windsurfing
or to develop one of those deep Mediterranean tans.

The resort is about one hour by car from Ajaccio and is well
situated for exploring the interior of the island and the spectacular
coast north towards Porto. However, public transport here, as
elsewhere on the island, is limited, so it is advisable to hire a car
for at least some of your stay.

EXCURSIONS
Two nearby villages are worth a mention . . . Cargèse, with its
charming white-washed architecture, which was a Greek
settlement; and Vico, tucked quietly into a mountain valley, and a
cool place to stop on a hot day's travelling. Another popular
excursion from Sagone is to the Gorge de la Spelunca.

USEFUL ADDRESSES

HOTELS
Cyrnos, tel. 95280001
U Risposu, tel. 952801121
Marine, on the beach, tel. 95280003
Santana, tel. 95280009

CAMPING
U Minta Strettu, tel. 95280186

HORSE RIDING
Ranch de Sagone, tel. 95280157

TENNIS
U Camarale, route de Vico, tel. 95280142

BANK
Crédit Agricole, tel. 95280244

SAINT-FLORENT

The regional capital of the Nebbio area set deep in a picture-postcard bay, Saint-Florent is one of Corsica's premier holiday resorts, particularly popular with yachtsmen and scuba divers. The town was built by the Genoese in the 1440s below a fine fortress tower, today the Gendarmerie, and kept its strategic value through Corsica's history of conquest. In 1793, when the conquerers were briefly English, Nelson was moved to declare 'Give me the gulf of St-Florent and two frigates, and not a single ship would leave Marseilles or Toulon,' – but he was never given a chance to prove his point. In the 18th and 19th centuries the town became neglected and almost depopulated because of the malaria-breeding marshlands round the river Aliso, but in the 20th century it has new life as a tourist magnet, the harbour having been enlarged for pleasure craft and hotels having sprung up along the road to Bastia.

Life in this extremely attractive resort is concentrated round its shaded central square, the harbour and the old streets that wind between tall houses of faded honey-grey along the water's edge.

The port itself is colourful, pretty and extremely animated in summer, lined as it is with restaurants and souvenir shops, while in the square, open-air diners and drinkers mingle with the strolling crowds.

A pebble beach stretches east along the bay, and to the west of the rocky river mouth lies a sandy beach.

Nearby Nebbio Cathedral, a handsome, 12th century Romanesque-Pisan building with some interesting carvings; the only remaining vestige of what was probably an impressive city, abandoned in the 16th century, it contains the relics of St Flor, a 3rd-century Roman martyr. To visit the cathedral one must ask for the key from the Syndicat d'Initiative.

EXCURSIONS
Close by the town is the village of Patrimonio, celebrated for its
excellent wines and for its remarkable 17th century church of
St-Martin, which boasts a huge and impressive bell-tower.

USEFUL ADDRESSES

TOURIST INFORMATION
Immeuble Sainte Anne, tel. 95370604

HOTELS
Bellevue, tel. 95370006
Auberge L'Europe, tel. 95370003
Madame Mere, tel. 95370274
Dolce Notte, road to Bastia, tel. 95370665 (a small, low-rise
    building with sea views from all bedrooms and an excellent
    restaurant)
Europa, Place des Portes, tel. 95370003
Tettola, tel. 95370853 (not in the centre of things, but a delightful
    little hotel bordering the sea).

CAMPING
Acqua Dolce, tel. 95370863
U Pezzo, tel. 95370165
Campo d'Olzo, tel. 95370334
Kalliste, tel. 95370308
La Pinede, tel. 95370726

RESTAURANTS
La Gaffe, on the port, tel. 95370012
La Crêperie, Place du Monument, tel. 95370852

BOAT HIRE
Corse Plaisance, tel. 95370058
Batelli Corsi, tel. 95370442
Locanautic, tel. 95370314

HORSE RIDING
'Ranch de Saint-Florent,' tel. 95370306

BANKS
Crédit Agricole, tel. 95370276

Société Générale, tel. 95370435

CAR HIRE
Avis, Ets Corse Plaisance, tel. 95370058
Citer, Garage Morati, tel. 95370519
Hertz, M. Canioni, Assureur, tel. 95370349
Locanautic, tel. 95370787

SANGUINAIRES ISLANDS

The tiny Sanguinaires islands, reached by boat from Ajaccio, are becoming increasingly popular holiday resorts, and now boast several excellent international-standard hotels. The Grande Sanguinaire is the longest of the four isles that constitute the archipelago, situated at the entrance to the Gulf of Ajaccio, and from here there is a splendid view of the gulf.

Boats depart twice daily in summer from the quay opposite Ajaccio's Place Maréchal Foch.

USEFUL ADDRESSES

HOTELS
Cala di Sole, tel. 95520136
Dolce Vita, tel. 95520093
Eden Roc, tel. 95520147
Isles Sanguinaires, tel. 95520252
Sun Beach, tel. 95215581
Stella di Mare, tel. 95520107

CAMPING
Pêch Barett, tel. 95520117

Sartène

Sartène rose to the status of a town by virtue of its involvement in the struggle between the local feudal patriarchs and outside attack, but unlike Corte, it lacks good natural defensive features, having been built on a slope overlooking the Rizzanese valley and the Gulf of Valinco. Its early history was punctuated by Barbarian attack from the sea, and the town was fortified in the 16th century.

Since it is situated on an important route between the uplands and coastal lowlands, migrant shepherds on their seasonal passage with the flocks used the town as a stage for the exchange of produce. While direct conflict with the Genoese was avoided. Sartène represented a consolidation, for the sake of security, of traditional land-owning patriarchal groups who had been conditioned throughout history to external threats. By the end of the 18th century the town had 1,200 inhabitants, mainly concerned with agriculture.

Sartène's austere medieval buildings are typically Coriscan, with flowered window boxes and garlands of washing brightening the sombre granite walls in the old town.

On Good Friday each year a three-hour long candlelit procession reconstitutes the various stages of the biblical climb to Calvary, along the granite steps of the old town. A man whose identity is kept secret represents Christ and leads the procession, dressed in a red robe, barefoot, chained, and carrying a heavy cross on his shoulder, his face and head hooded. The vicar of Sartène makes the choice and is the only person to know the identity of the man. In the past it could have been a bandit or criminal seeking atonement for his misdeeds.

PLACES OF INTEREST

Church of Ste-Marie
An imposing granite church, it contains the cross and chains carried by the Grand Penitent during the penitential procession.

Museum of Prehistoric Corsica
Dominating the town and housed in an ancient prison dating from 1843, the museum contains artefacts dating from the early Mediterranean Neolithic period (6,000 BC) to the early Iron Age. A tableau traces the history of Corsica and its inhabitants, with numerous photographs of archaeological sites, statues and menhirs.

Hôtel De Ville
The ancient palace of the Genoese governors, located in the old

town. The steps immediately to the left lead directly to the marriage room.

Place De La Liberation
Formerly known as place Porta, this is an attractive square lined with cafés and a market, and is the most animated centre of the town, where all the Sartènais meet.

Nearby
Palaggiu megaliths   258 menhirs, the largest single group in the Mediterranean.
Tizzano   a little holiday resort and marina offering an attractive beach, creeks and scuba diving possibilities.
Belvedere de Foce   located 5 km away, offering a splendid view of the gulf of Valinco.

USEFUL ADDRESSES

TOURIST INFORMATION
Rue Borgo, tel. 95770537

HOTELS
Les Roches, tel. 95770761
Villa Piano, road to Propriano, tel. 95770704

CAMPING
L'Avena, tel. 95770218
Olva les Eucalyptus, tel. 95771158

RESTAURANTS
La Chaumiere, 39 rue Med-Cap Benedetti, tel. 95770713
U San Damianu, Av San-Nicolao, tel. 95771477

TRAVEL AGENCY
Ollandini, rue Gabriel-Péri, tel. 95771841

CAR HIRE
Avis, Cours Soeur-Amelie, tel. (95) 770504

HORSE RIDING
Centre Equestre d'A Madunina, tel. 95771137

BANKS
Caisse d'Epargne P.T.T., tel. 95770112
Crédit Agricole, immeuble la Résidence, tel. 95770732
Crédit Lyonnais, rue Sainte Anne, tel. 95770196
Société Générale, rue Tafani, tel. 95770257

Sisco

The little coastal village of Sisco, which boasts a small marina
among its many attractions, was a commune of metal workers in
the Middle Ages. At nearby Balba the church of St-Martin
contains a famous hidden treasury including a saint's skull encased
in silver-gilt. For a chance to see it you must enquire at the house of
the curé.

USEFUL ADDRESSES

HOTEL
La Marine, tel. 95352104

CAMPING
La Casajola, tel. 95352150
Le Renajo, tel. 95352114

Solenzara

Until quite recently Solenzara was simply a small, pretty fishing
village on Corsica's east coast. Today, the village is undergoing
considerable touristic development. Much of it, alas, of detriment
to its enormous natural charm and appeal. Ugly and incongruous
blocks of flats have been erected on a prime site by the beach, and
more along the main road. This apart, Solenzara has all the
ingredients of a splendid little holiday resort, including not one but
two excellent beaches and an attractive new yachting harbour
which was being expanded further during my last visit. It is well
equipped for windsurfers, and is also a popular base for deep-sea
fishing, water-skiing and skin-diving.

The main street is lined with a good selection of bars, cafés, crêperies, pizzerias and restaurants, together with supermarkets to provide for the increasing numbers of self-catering holidaymakers.

Solenzara's appeal is greatly enhanced by the fact that it is an excellent base from which to explore the wonderful scenery on the eastern coast of Corsica and for making an excursion through the incredible and very beautiful Bavella Pass.

USEFUL ADDRESSES

TOURIST INFORMATION
Mairie annexe, tel. 95574151

HOTELS
La Solenzara, tel. 95574218 (a pleasant, two-star hotel with a
    pretty garden and nicely appointed rooms)
Le Maquis et Mer, tel. 95574007
Mare e Festa, tel. 95574291
A Staffa, tel. 95574246

CAMPING
Côte des Nacres, tel. 95574065

RESTAURANT
Caravelle, tel. 95574627

CAR HIRE
CITER, Garage Planelles, tel. 95574226

BOAT HIRE
Cofamarine, marina, tel. 95574001

SKIN DIVING
Subaquatic-Club de la Côtes des Nacres, Camping des Nacres,
    tel. 95574615

HORSE RIDING
'Alpa' Poney Club de Solenzara, tel. 95574182

BANKS
Société Général, tel. 95574251
Crédit Agricole, tel. 95574577

Tarco

Tarco is one of the smaller and quieter resorts on Corsica. It is located on the east coast, just north of Pinarello, and has one of the best beaches on the island, a lovely stretch of sand overlooked by the wooded slopes of the mountains.

The village has a modest choice of bars and restaurants, but the bright lights of Porto Vecchio are only a few kilometres away for those who feel like a night on the town. Hiring a car is advisable unless one is looking for a really idle holiday.

USEFUL ADDRESSES

CAMPING
Campo Tarco, tel. 95714285
Le Bon Anno, tel. 955722135

RESTAURANT
La Taverna 'A Marina', tel. 95572001

Tiuccia

The small resort of Tiuccia is spread along a fine sandy beach on the Gulf of Sagone, overlooked by the crumbling ruins of Capraja Castle, the home of the Cinarca family, once the most powerful in the land.

Few families anywhere in the world have had a more turbulent history, and although the setting for the ruins could scarcely be more peaceful, there is a lurking sense of oppression as though the ghosts of the Cinarchesi are still tied to the scene of so much bloodshed, treachery and tragedy.

USEFUL ADDRESSES

HOTELS
Cinarca, tel. 95522139
La Liscia, tel. 95282140

Club San Sebastiano, tel. 95522035
Castel d'Orcino, tel. 95522063

RESTAURANT
Les Flots Bleus, tel. 95522165

Venaco

Venaco is a very pleasant mountain village with houses
dramatically perched, almost defying the laws of gravitation, and is
popular with holidaymakers who prefer quiet, inland resorts to
those on the coast.

USEFUL ADDRESSES

HOTELS
Du Torrent, tel. 95470018, Du Bosquet, tel. 95470011, and Calme
　　et Repos, tel. 95470320, all in St Pierre-de-Venaco.

HORSE RIDING
'A Staffa', Centre de Randonnées Equestres de Venaco,
　　tel. 95470013 or 95470201

Vico

Vico is an attractive little inland centre, popular with those who
prefer the country to the seaside, and among its attractions is the
Caldanelle Thermal Spring Company whose waters are said to be
beneficial in the treatment of dermatitis.

USEFUL ADDRESSES

HOTEL
U Paradisa, rte du Couvent, tel. 95266162

CAMPING
La Sposata, tel. 95266155

BANKS
Banque Populaire Provençale et Corse, tel. 95263604

Vivario

At an altitude of 650 metres, Vivario is popular in summer with
lovers of the outdoors, and becomes a ski resort in winter, with
12 km of pistes, while in the environs it is possible to fish for trout
in the Vecchio, or shoot pigeons.

Of interest is the fountain in the town's central square, and the
ruins of the Fort de Parciola: located on the road to Corte at an
altitude of 792 metres, it was built about 1770 by the French to
reinforce that at Vizzavona, and was subsequently turned into a
prison.

EXCURSIONS
Various fascinating excursions are possible from Vivario, with
excellent views from the Pont du Vecchio, 4.5 km to the north.
Particularly popular are trips to Ghisoni and to the Col de Sorba,
one of the highest passes on the island; when the weather is clear
the view from here of the valley of the Vecchio and of Monte d'Oro
is magnificent.

USEFUL ADDRESSES

HOTEL
Macchia e Monti, tel. 95472092

CAMPING
Camping de Savaggio, tel. 95472007

Zonza

A mountainous village, 2,500 feet above sea level, Zonza is beautifully sited among chestnut groves and striking mountain scenery. A favourite resort with trout fishermen and hikers, it is an excellent base for exploring the Bavella Pass, which cuts through the mountain chain to provide one of the most spectacular landscapes on the island. The granite needles of Bavella rear above a plateau covered with grass and sparsely strewn with windswept pines. To the north stretches the Incudine Massif, while to the east the sea is framed between walls of red rock. With luck, visitors may catch a glimpse of a flock of moufflons on the rocky slopes.

Of interest is the Moorish influence in Zonza's restaurants, with dishes such as 'Brique à l'oeuf' more commonly associated with North African countries.

USEFUL ADDRESSES

HOTELS
Incudine, tel. 95784276
La Terrasse, tel. 95784242

RESTAURANT
La Terrasse, tel. 95784242

USEFUL INFORMATION

'If you look like your passport photo, then in all probability you need the journey.'

WHEN TO GO TO CORSICA

The nature of Corsica's topography gives the island a wide range of climatic variations. Visitors tend to think in the first place of its hot dry Mediterranean summer and its rainy autumn, and indeed the winter temperatures in the coastal regions of Corsica, averaging 14°C, are distinctly higher than in Britain or the fashionable south of France. At the height of the summer, in spite of Corsica's insular situation, it can be very hot, so the best time for a visit is May, June or September. Spring comes to the south coast as early as the end of February or the beginning of March.

Statistics for the low-lying regions most frequented by tourists quote average daytime temperature in December and January as 14°C rising to 16°C in May and reaching a peak of 23°C in July and August, sometimes prolonged to September. The autumn is considerably warmer than spring, with October and even November recording higher temperatures than May.

Rainfall is sharply divided into two seasons, far more predictable than in northern climes; the major falls occur in October and November, with a lesser percipitation in March, while a rainless season is an accepted feature of summer.

The springing up of a sudden wind, a hazard in many Mediterranean countries, presents a danger to those out in small boats, and in the dry summer months these winds can, and do, threaten the island's superb forests – with devastating, sweeping fires.

From the sandy beaches to a height of 200 metres, the classical Mediterranean climate prevails. Most of the villages lie in the 'intermediary' zone from 200 to 900 metres where the chestnut trees flourish. Climbing to 1,500 metres, the summers are still warm though subject to short periods of rain, while the winters, invariably cold, may find the inhabitants under snow from December to March. Above 1,500 metres the scene is pure Alpine. Many roads in the mountains may be impassable from October until May. In summer heat, however, the cooler climate of the mountainous regions of the interior can be very agreeable.

TEMPERATURE GUIDE (°C)

Jan	Feb	Mar	Apr	May	Jun	Jul	Aug	Sep	Oct	Nov	Dec
12.9	12.2	14.1	16.5	21.0	25.5	28.1	27.9	25.7	21.5	18.1	14.5

HOW TO GET TO CORSICA

BY AIR

Air France, British Airways and others operate one-stop scheduled flights to Corsica: Ajaccio, Bastia, Calvi and Figari being the main airports served, together with the smaller one at Propriano.

ADDRESSES

Air France: 158 New Bond Street, London W1Y 0AY, tel. 01-499 9511
British Airways, West London Air Terminal, Cromwell Road, London SW7 4ED, tel. 01-897 4000

BY SEA

SNCM (Société Nationale Maritime Corse Mediteranée) operates a daily ferry service during the high season and twice weekly in winter from Marseilles, Nice and Toulon to Ajaccio, Bastia, Calvi, Ile-Rousse and Propriano. The crossing takes between five and ten hours, and summer crossings should be booked well in advance because of the demand. Reductions offered on fares are similar to those of French Railways. The trip from Nice to Ile-Rousse is the shortest, and that from Marseilles to Bastia the longest. In the period between October and mid-May 30 % discounts are offered for those aged under 25, 50% for those aged over 60, and other reductions. Interrail card holders are given a 33% discount. For crossings from Nice only, the 30% discount for ages under 26 applies throughout the year. Crossings to Corsica from Italy are shorter and about the same price. (Check with your travel agent for the latest details).

ADDRESS: Continental Shipping (SNCM), 179 Piccadilly, London W1Y 0BA, tel. 01-491 4968

Corsica Ferries operates mid-June until early September to Bastia from Livorno, La Spezia and Savona, and serves Calvi and Savona four times a week from mid-June to the beginning of September and less often at the beginning of June and the end of September.

NAV.AR.MA runs from Livorno and Piombino to Bastia from April to the middle of October, including a daily service in summer.

TRAVELLING AROUND

BY CAR
One of the best ways of seeing Corsica is by car, and all the major car rental companies are well represented; many of them, together with their addresses and telephone numbers, are indicated in the various resort descriptions contained in this guide.

Fly/drive arrangements are available through airlines and tour operators, a list of which can be obtained from the French National Tourist Office. Most companies offer weekly rates with unlimited mileage which works out cheaper. 'Super Saver' weekly rates with unlimited mileage have to be prebooked in the UK with a minimum of 24 hours' notice, although some companies require a minimum of seven clear days. A refundable deposit for possible damage is required, and extra insurance is usually advised, while an optional CDW (Collision Damage Waiver) is available from most companies. The minimum age to hire a car is 18 years, but some companies have raised this limit to 21 or 23 years; the upper age limit is usually 60 to 65.

For those who prefer to arrange car hire before they leave, here is a list of several major car rental companies and their offices in the UK:
Avis Rent-a-Car, Trident House, Station Road, Hayes, Middlesex, tel. 01-848 8733
Budget Rent-a-Car International, International House, 85 Great North Road, Hatfield, Herts AL8 7QU, tel. (Linkline) 0800 5050
Godfrey Davis Europcar, Bushey House, High Street, Bushey, Watford, Herts, tel. (central reservations) 01-950 5050

Hertz Rent-a-Car, Radnor House, 1272 London Road, Norbury, London SW16, tel. 01–670 1799

BY BUS
Coach services call at Corsican villages generally once daily, main itineraries starting from the principal towns of Ajaccio, Bastia, Calvi, Ile-Rousse, Corte, Sartène and Porto-Vecchio. A number of companies operate excursions varying in length from half-a-day to seven days.

BY RAIL
Corsican Railways provides links with the main towns of Ajaccio, Corte, Bastia, Ile-Rousse and Calvi, travelling over 232 km of the most picturesque country, a scenic journey winding through mountains, on high viaducts over great valleys, and diving into tunnels. There are regular daily services, Ajaccio-Bastia and return, a three hour trip, frequencies being increased during the peak summer season.

Between Calvi and Ile-Rousse as many as 30 trains a day provide easy access to the numerous beaches dotting the coast. The Corsican railway system accepts the Interrail Pass, offering a 50% reduction.

PASSPORTS AND VISAS

British Nationals need only a valid passport for travel to Corsica: either a full British Passport, valid ten years; or a British Visitor's Passport, valid for one year.

ACCOMMODATION

Hotels in Corsica, in the main, are not as sophisticated as in many more highly developed holiday islands – and, in this respect, neighbouring Sardinia probably has the edge. However, a large number of Corsican hotels have been built comparatively recently, and have good facilities. At the last count the island offered approximately 28,000 hotel beds, and there are five grades, from one to four star luxe. Very few single rooms are available, but you normally pay only around 30% extra for a third bed, while many hotel chains offer a free bed for a child under 12 in the same room as the parents. Room and all meals, that is full-board or pension terms, are usually offered for a stay of three days or longer. Half board or demi-pension (room, breakfast and one meal) terms are usually available outside the peak holiday period and some hotels offer this in season too, although very many Corsican hotels do not have restaurants and consequently offer room only, or bed and breakfast arrangements.

Hotels are mainly situated along the coast, but efforts have been made to encourage their development further inland, and with some success. During the high season visitors are advised to reserve their rooms in advance, whether they be on the coast or inland. A *'Guide to Hotels'* is published each year by l'Agence Regionale du Tourisme et des Loisirs, 22 Cours Grandval 20176, Ajaccio.

CAMPING
Corsica extends a particular welcome to compers, with a wide variety of camp sites in the mountains, the forests, and along the coasts. About 30,000 campers can be accommodated in the sites, and many new ones open each year. A guide to registered camp/caravan sites is published each year by l'Agence Regionale du Tourisme in Ajaccio (for address see above).

HOLIDAY VILLAGES
About 50 holiday villages offer various stays at inclusive prices, and include facilities for preparing meals and the use of facilities for leisure, sporting and cultural activities. Some are reserved for naturists.

'GÎTES RURAUX'
The 'gîte rural' is a fully furnished house situated close to a farm or village. In compliance with the Charter of 'Gîtes de France,' it is graded according to the degree of comfort and quality of its surroundings. The 'gîtes ruruax' in Corsica offer accommodation for approximately 1,187.

EATING AND DRINKING

On the whole, Corsican cuisine is not up to the standards of the French mainland nor, for that matter, neighbouring Sardinia, though they both suffer as islands from having to import many of the basic ingredients. Corsican restaurants tend to be expensive by the standards of most holiday destinations, but the countless pizzerias that have sprung up of late – there now seems to be at least one in every village, and scores in the main resorts – usually provide less expensive pizza-and-pasta-style dishes.

The 'touristic' cuisine itself is usually an amalgam of French Provençal, Italian, Spanish and local, meaning that those with an appreciation of these various cuisines are unlikely to be disappointed.

As far as ethnic food is concerned, Corsican charcuterie tends to be more robust and more savoury than that of mainland France or Italy, though somewhat similar to that of Sardinia. *Saliccio*, peppery and highly-spiced sausage, is more meaty, less fatty, than most mainland equivalents.

The pigs that run wild through the maquis provide the raw material for excellent *prisuttu* (the Corsican version of prosciutto ham), *lonzu* (rolled and smoked fillet of pork) and *figatelli*, a black, smoked pork sausage. Roast leg of lamb, kid and suckling pig, are also very good.

Corsican game is also good and comparatively plentiful, though like wildlife everywhere it is threatened by too many guns. The becasse, or woodcock, is a delicacy, especially when served on toast, or stuffed with paté de foie.

One dish the visitor is likely to encounter on most restaurant menus is sanglier, or wild boar, often cooked with brandy and red wine; it can compare favourably with the best. Partridge is another popular dish, though the birds are becoming increasingly rare.

Many of the island's cheeses are made from goats' and ewes' milk, which gives them a rather exotic flavour. *Brocciu*, a cheese made from a mixture of whey and whole milk, is an important ingredient in Corsican cooking, adding flavour to soup, cakes, turnovers and fritters, as well as pasta dishes, and is often served on its own to round-off a meal. Other noteworthy cheeses are the soft varieties of *Calenzana, Niolo* and *Venaco*, and the pressed cheeses of Sartène. There is also a delicious blue cheese, *Ponte-Lecchia*.

It is natural that, being an island, fish should feature heavily on

Corsican menus. Unfortunately it is not particularly cheap, especially shellfish, although there is a reasonably wide choice, from loup de mer, red mullet, pageot, and expensive langouste or crayfish. Trout can also be encountered in many restaurants, as can fish soup and moules (mussels), cooked in a variety of ways.

The staple diet of the people used to be polenta, a flour made from chestnuts growing throughout the island, and though less common it is still used today in many forms, especially for desserts, cakes and fritters. Chestnuts are also served whole as a vegetable, and go particularly well with boiled fennel.

WINES

Corsican wines, while lacking distinction, are certainly satisfying for anyone looking for 'body'. The most popular tends to be the rosé, a good companion to a meal on a warm summer day. White wines are relatively rare, although Cap Corse produces perfectly acceptable white wines under the appellation *Côteaux du Cap Corse*. On the coasts of Ajaccio, red wines are favoured, while on the south of the island, under the appellation *Porto Vecchio*, and *Figari Pianotoli*, one finds red, white and rosé wines. Those produced on the coast between Bastia and Solenzara, and the region of Ponte-Lecchia, are fruity and of high quality.

The producers of wine and their professional organisations, supported by the authorities, have marked out a route designed to enable visitors to discover the vintage wines. An explanatory leaflet available free of charge from tourist information offices gives a selection of addresses of those who grow and bottle some of the traditional wines.

SHOPS AND SHOPPING

Banks are normally open from 09.00 until noon and again from 14.00 until 16.00 weekdays, and closed either Saturdays or Mondays; they also close early on the day before a bank holiday.

Post Offices are usually open from 08.00 until 19.00 during the week, and from 08.00 to noon on Saturdays; while food shops usually open from 07.00 to 18.30 or 19.30, and other shops from 09.00 to 18.30 or 19.30. Many shops close all or half day on Mondays, while some food shops, especially bakers, open on Sunday mornings. In many regions of Corsica shops close from noon until 14.00.

RIVER FISHING

Corsica has so many delightful rivers considering the size of the island that it is an angler's paradise. All the visiting fisherman needs to do is to join one of the many local *assistations*, the addresses of which can be obtained from: Fédération Départementale de Pêche et de Pisciculture, 7 blvd Paoli, 20200 Bastia, tel. 95314731; Fédération Inter-Départementale de Pêche et de Pisciculture, 13 rue Docteur-Del-Pellegrino, 20000 Ajaccio, tel. 95231332

HORSE RIDING

Corsica is excellently equipped for those who enjoy horse riding and pony trekking, with more than 1,000 km of suitable trails, often ancient mule paths or sheep grazing trails, and many cutting through breathtaking mountain or coastal scenery. Most of the major holiday resorts have equestrian centres of varying degrees of sophistication, but for more information contact the relevant local tourist information office or the riding centres themselves. Various packaged itineraries are available, some involving hotel accommodation, others 'gîtes', and there are even those where riders sleep out in the open in sheep pens.

HUNTING

Game is abundant throughout the island, and hunting is a popular activity, practised from the first Sunday in September until the first Sunday in January, with the following exceptions: duck shooting open until 15 February, other water fowl until 28 February; woodcocks until 28 Feburary, wood pigeon until 31 March; and thrush and blackbird shooting until 28 February.

For further information contact: Fédération Départementale des Chasseurs de la Corse-du-Sud, 19 Av Beverini, 20000 Ajaccio, tel. 95231691; Fédération Départementale des Chasseurs de Haute-Corse, résidence Nouvelle-Corniche St-Joseph, 20200 Bastia, tel. 953222599.

SAILING

Corsica is admirably suited for sailing holidays; situated 170 km from the French mainland, 83 km from the Italian peninsula and 12 km from Sardinia, it forms the crossroads of pleasure sailing in the western Mediterranean. With over 1,000 km of coastline along which are dotted a succession of well equipped ports (3,200 berths) and unspoilt bays, Corsica is also a paradise for coastal sailing.

Harmoniously arranged in the main coastal resorts of the island, sailing and skin diving clubs offer a wide variety of activities designed to satisfy the keenest enthusiast.

SARDINIA

'One of the most neglected spots in Europe'

ARTHUR YOUNG

CONSIDERING THAT, AFTER Sicily, Sardinia is the largest island in the Mediterranean, it remains relatively undiscovered as a holiday destination, at least by the masses. Big touristic developments have taken place over the years, notably in areas such as the Costa Smeralda on the northeastern tip of the island, but on the whole Sardinia is a comparatively peaceful, 'up-market' holiday island, with a particular appeal to the wealthier, older generation and those looking for something other than the usual mass-market holiday destination.

The Sardinians themselves, a short, dark, good-looking race, consider themselves distinct from Italians, and the mainland seems much farther away than it really is, both because of the island's independent spirit and its semi-autonomy.

Sardinia is famous for its near pocket-sized donkeys, handsome, intricate native costumes, pastas, brooding mountain areas, highly distinctive, artistic woven baskets, and its legions of fine, sandy beaches. Some argue that the island lacks Italy's exuberance, but it is certainly popular with mainland Italians themselves, including increasing numbers of younger Italians, with the result that lively bars and discothèques are opening up apace to cater for their needs.

However, Sardinia also has a special appeal for the adventurous traveller, for those who enjoy touring holidays, and for campers, with a variety of scenery and sights so great that something new, compelling, attractive or awesome is bound to turn up around almost every curve of the road.

An autonomous special statute region of insular Italy, formed of an island bearing the same name and of numerous minor isles forming a crown, among which are Asinara, La Maddalena, Caprera, San Pietro and Sant'Antioco, Sardinia is washed by the

Tyrrhenian Sea to the east, the Sardinian Sea to the west, and the Mediterranean Sea to the south, being separated from Corsica to the north by the strait of Bonifacio.

Rectangular in shape, the island's irregular relief is formed by a series of mountainous groups (Limbara, Gennargentu, Sarrabus) culminating at 1834 metres in the Punta La Marmora of the Gennargentu massif; in the south-westerly sector. Between the Gennargentu and the reliefs of the Iglesiente, stretches the Campidano alluvial plain.

The very indented coastlines; rich in coves, soft sandy shores and caves, are faced by numerous islands. Of particular interest are the inland areas which show unique environmental characteristics in the Mediterranean combined with an unpolluted nature. The water courses (Flumendosa, Coghinas, Tirso, Flumini Mannu, Cedrino, Cixerri) are of a torrent-like character and are almost all dammed forming artificial basins used for the production of electric power and for the irrigation of vast areas.

Handicrafts have a centuries-old tradition on the island and are still widely practised. Among the vast range of the items produced, the rugs, tapestries, blankets, embroidery, baskets, carved wood and pieces of pottery are particularly admired.

The nature, position of the island, small number of coastal resorts in comparison to the towns inland, and the historic events, have for long periods favoured the isolation of the Sardinian population, permitting the autonomous development of their lives and reducing to a minimum the external influences; continuity exists in the landscape and in the customs and traditions of the people.

More than 7,000 constructions known as *nuraghi* constitute a testimony to the great Bronze Age local civilisation. Some of these constructions are second in size only to the Pyramids, while pre-nuraghic inhabitants left behind impressive funeral and magic monuments such as the *domus de janas*, *perdas fittas*, *tombas de gigantes*, megalithic enclosures with sacrificial altars, or magic circles, rather Celtic than Mediterranean in their inspiration.

All testify to the fact that Sardinia is a great melting pot of peoples and cultures coming from the north and from the south, from the east and from the west. This is not only true for ancient history: Phoenicians, Carthaginians, Romans, Byzantines, Vandals, Saracens, Pisans, Genoese, Aragonese, Spaniards, Piedmontese and even Austrians have all left their imprints, particularly evident at Nora, Tharros, the 'Tophet' of

110

Sant'Antioco, the Carthaginian fortresses of the Sulcis, the medieval towers of Cagliari and Oristano, the Castle of Bosa, the Aragonese bastions of Alghero, right up to the 'liberty style' architecture of the Piazza d'Italia at Sassari.

Then there are the churches and the basilicas, with their Romanic-Pisan style, such as that of Saccargia and dozens of others: stone jewels set into the silent country roads; the houses of the Campidano, repeating the plan of the ancient Roman dwellings; and those of the hill shepherds which faithfully reproduce the peculiar building techniques of the Sardinians.

That Sardinia is a huge reservoir of cultures can be seen from the shepherds at work or, better still, at play, when they improvise love poems or serenades, when they dance to the rhythm of the harsh, but at the same time, harmonious vocal tunes, marking the rhythm without any instrument. Sards dance in couples when the dance is erotic or in large circles when the dance is ritual, the magic chain reinforcing the contact of man with the spirits of nature.

Just beyond the modern capital of Cagliari the peasant tradition of the island lives and prospers . . . fresh, cool houses with Spanish-style patios, flowered balconies, intricate wrought iron work, splendid jewels of Phoenician workmanship, songs and popular dances, poems, competitions and wine.

The flux of different peoples, customs, work methods and traditions to Sardinia was bound to create an original and multifarious craftmanship. It is impossible to illustrate all the examples of artistic Sardinian handicrafts that range from furnishings to clothing, from work tools to hobby objects, but the Sards use leather, wool (dyed with herbs and molluscs), cotton, reeds, chaff, daffodil, dwarf palm, chalk and kaolin, wood cork and coral as material to create artefacts.

Then there are the carpets and tapestries, differing from area to area, and belonging to schools of art with ancient traditions: baskets, chests, cotton and woollen quilts embroidered as in ancient times; wrought iron and wood motifs and observations of country life.

Folklore, too, lives and flourishes in Sardinia, as the great island feasts testify. Visitors who want to experience this at first hand should go the Feast of St Efisio at Cagliari, of the Redeemer at Nuoro, the 'Cavalcata Sarda' at Sassari, the 'Sartiglia' at Oristano, the 'barefoot running' of St Salvatore at Cabras, or the 'Ardia' at Sedilo. They should see how they trim up the ox pairs of the Patron's coach, or enter the little smoky taverns and listen to the wine drinkers; or wait until the High Mass is over during the great religious festivities to appreciate the grace and dignity with which older and younger women still wear their colourful costumes rich in fiery reds, saffron ribbons, soft blues and broom yellow.

The visitor to Sardinia should not look for a typically Sardinian gastronomy, with the exception of meat, because the central position of the island in the Mediterranean and the crossing of peoples and civilizations have produced culinary customs of Spanish, Italian, North African and Provençal origin, creating an unusual mixture of dishes . . . fish soup (boullabaisse); couscous, meat paella, delicious roast fish, lobsters, sea food, excellent pastas, fresh cheese ravioli, 'malloreddus,' a sort of dumpling made of hard wheat and yellowed with saffron, as well as many other Mediterranean dishes.

Topography and history have combined to divide Sardinia rather neatly into four provincial regions – Cagliari, Nouro, Oristano and Sassari – each fascinating in its own way and boasting many lovely, uncluttered beaches, little fishing villages, mountain resorts, ancient towns and historic excavations.

CAGLIARI

The entire southern part of Sardinia, comprising the broad plain of Campidano, with the mountains of Sette Fratelli, Serpeddi and Sarrabus to the east, and Mount Linas and the Sulcitano massif to the west, constitutes the province of Cagliari, occupying a surface area of 7,125 sq km. The eastern and western coasts, from Porto Corallo as far as Capo Frasca – a chain of sandy beaches and rocky cliffs – are washed by a glittering sea, well enough stocked with fish, and the climate is mild in winter and hot in summer, though sufficiently tempered by light breezes as to offer good bathing from May to October.

The history of the province as a whole was always closely linked with that of Cagliari itself and it was struggled over, with varying success, by the Carthaginians, the Romans, Byzantines, Arabs, Pisans, Aragonese and Savoyards. Its 3,000 year history has roots in prehistory and in the great civilization of the earliest Sardinians, the Nuraghic era, whose most important remains are seen in the small bronzes of the period and the megalithic complex of 'Su Nuraxi' at Barumini.

The province offers various interests and attractions for the visitor, ranging from poetry, culture, art, history and archaeology to the innate hospitality of its people. A noteworthy feature, of some rarity elsewhere, is the presence of a breed of dwarf horses, in a wild state, which can be seen on the basalt plateau of the Giari, near Tulli, Gesturi and Genoni.

Of the numerous caves in Cagliari, that at San Giovanni, near Domusnovas is one of the most impressive, while the province shows its imaginative side in an immense heritage of folklore, its most characteristic feature being the resplendent, many-coloured costumes. Displays and exhibitions take place in countless centres throughout the year, while in some communities (Sinnai, Sant' Antioco, Cagliari, Teulada, Assemini) local handicrafts are popular, such as carpets, tapestries, ceramics, terracotta, goldsmith's work and inlaid wood.

In many towns and villages delicious food can be savoured, usually a simple affair enhanced by sturdy wines with an unmistakeable bouquet, and followed by tasty cakes. In the centres of Maracalagonis, Sinnai and Sestu, visitors will often find that evening meals are accompanied by traditional island dances and songs.

SASSARI

The province of Sassari, the nearest part of Sardinia to Corsica and continental Europe, comprises the entire northern part of the island, from Villanova Monteleone and Alghero on the western coast as far as Olbia and Porto San Paulo on the eastern coast, and the islands of Asinar, the Maddalena archipelago, Tavolara, Molara and other smaller islands.

Fast, modern ships link Toulon, Genoa and Civitavecchia with Porto Torres; Bonifacio (Corsica) with St. Teresa di Gallura; Genoa, Leghorn and Civitavecchia with Olbia; and Civitavecchia with Golfo Aranci. The airports of Alghero and Olbia are linked directly, or by easy connections, with the rest of the world.

Many centres of interest to the holidaymaker and visitor are located within this, Italy's biggest province, from the sunswept beaches of white sand to the granite cliff faces scooped out by the winds and the chalky scarps and fantastic marine grottos, and the clear sea and scented pinewoods.

This is a Sardinia which changes without losing sight of its ancient traditions. Between the heady perfume of coastal brushwood to the air of the mountain woodlands, there are many traces of the peoples who possessed the land across the centuries. In addition to ancient monuments, churches and fortifications, there are the nuraghic buildings dating back more than a thousand years, and the relics of the 'giudicale' period.

The coast, no less than the interior, offers considerable interest . . . handicrafts, sporting centres (for sailing particularly), tasty and simple cooking, popular traditions, leisure resorts, cultural events; all of which make splendid excuses for a holiday here. Hotel facilities and tourist accommodation in the province are modern and diverse, from the most luxurious and sophisticated hotels to family-style pensions; there are about 19,000 beds throughout 700 km of coastline, with 11,000 in camping sites, tourist villages and youth hostels as well as holiday homes.

All this can be enjoyed in a mild climate prevailing throughout almost the entire year.

NOURO

The mountainous province of Nouro, with a surface area of 7043,92 sq km, and its epicentre in the Gennargentu massif, occupies the central part of Sardinia, comprising within its territory Baronia, Ogliastra, Sarcidano, Mandrolisai, Planargia, Marghine, Barbagia, subdivided into Barbagia di Ollolai, Belvi and Seulo. Its configuration is varied and rugged, owing to sudden upheavals: mountains, plateaux of varying natures and extent, alternating with deep valleys, with Punta Lamarmora, in the Gennargentu massif, the island's highest summit, at 1,834 metres.

The coasts, extending from San Teodoro as far as Tertenia to the east, and from Bosa as far as Magomadas to the west, are not heavily indented, but in general are rocky and deep-bottomed, except for the coves of Bosa and the broad gulf of Orosei. The sea, which dashes against the cliffs and beats on the fine white beaches with its crystalline water, provides a magnificent setting to a landscape of broad stretches of dark green, heavily strewn with flowers, granite mountains, oak woods and ilex groves.

The climate of Nouro is typically Mediterranean, becoming milder in the coastal regions through the softening effects of the sea. In the mountains the winter can be hard and severe, with heavy snowfalls.

Little is known of the region's primitive inhabitants, but

evidence of prehistoric occupation is indicated by various local finds. The Nuraghic civilization is particularly ancient, taking its name from the characteristic buildings known as 'nuraghi', many of which are to be found in the Marghine and Nuoroese districts particularly. No less ancient are the *Tombe dei Giganti* and the *Pozzi Sacri*, witnesses of a culture still clouded in mystery.

The Province of Nuoro boasts fine handicraft traditions of various types: benches of inlaid walnut or chestnut; woven woollen cloths of different colours and adapted to various uses such as carpets, tapestries and blankets; leatherwork, ceramics (Dorgali), baskets (Ollolai, Olzai and in the Planargia area), goldsmith's work and silver filigree.

The numerous festivals held throughout the year in all the provincial centres offers the visitor the opportunity to admire the magnificent, brightly coloured costumes which represent one of the area's principal attractions.

ORISTANO

The territory of the province of Oristano comprises many geographical elements characterising the island's morphology: the gulf of Oristano, ancient capital of the Giudicato d'Arborea, halfway along the eastern coast and the centre of a contraction marked on the edges of the basaltic Capo S. Marco and Capo della Frasca; the remote peninsula of Sinis; the numerous neighbouring pools, with canals, dunes and wildlife of great interest; Monte Ferru, with its characteristic woods; and the oasis of green at S. Leonardo and Santu Lussurgiu.

Around Oristano, founded in the 11th century by the inhabitants of Tharros and one of the most outstanding political and cultural centres in medieval Sardinia, are many towns characterized by a common history. The archaeological heritage and the monumental remains are not isolated episodes, but form part of single context, created not only by an enlightened political and cultural activity but also by the common struggle of men against the elements and against natural disasters. Its period of maximum splendour coincided with its spell of independence during the 13th and 14th centuries.

During the centuries of Spanish domination, famines and plagues marked the life of Oristano; nowadays the province is effectively part of the Sardinian 'renaissance', characterized by pastoral-agricultural activity and small industries, while the local gastronomy is linked principally with fishing.

RECOMMENDED RESORTS

UNLIKE CORSICA, which has numerous well-known and well-developed holiday resorts scattered about its shores, especially on its west coast, Sardinia has comparatively few; but what it may lack in quantity it certainly does not lack in quality.

COSTA SMERALDA

Undisputed queen of the Sardinian holiday scene is the up-market Costa Smeralda, a resort area between Golfo degli Aranci and Arzachena, on Sardinia's east coast. The area, developed over the past 20 years or so by the Aga Khan and associates, is extremely popular with the rich and status-seekers on package tours. At its centre is Porto Cervo, whose recently-built Stella Maris church has a painting by El Greco. Amenities are in keeping with the fame the resort has acquired: an extensive marina, the 18-hole Pevero golf course only ten minutes away, and facilities for all types of water sports. For those looking for sophisticated, up-market accommodation, this is the place to be. One of the most successful hotels is the Pitrizzia, a cluster of cottages in a forest setting. The Cala di Volpe and Romazzioni hotels are also highly rated by up-market visitors, while Porto Cervo itself boasts the Hotel Cervo, right at the centre of things, and with the atmosphere of an elegant but informal club.

ALGHERO

Less expensive than the Costa Smeralda, and more heavily featured in travel companies' programmes, is Alghero, an

117

attractive, lively town with a distinctive Spanish flavour, and a particular favourite with British holidaymakers.

Located on the fertile plain of Sardinia's west coast, Alghero, in a sense, is not a Sardinian town at all. Founded by the Arabs and controlled by Genoa in the Middle Ages, the Aragonese found it a valuable and strategic site, and began their Sardinia conquest with Alghero's annexation in 1355. Alghero's past is readily visible to the visitor, the town having the appearance of being built for noblemen; and this suits it perfectly for its modern role as a town geared for tourists.

North of the resort a huge sandy beach runs for several kilometres, and tourist facilities are excellent; with a splendid range of hotels, from the elegant five-star Villa Las Trovas, located in an old palace and with its own private beach, to more modest hotels such as the Eleonora; restaurants, cafés and evening entertainments, as well as numerous interesting churches and historic sites for if you weary of the sun.

SANTA MARGHERITA DI PULA

One of the biggest and most successful holiday developments in Sardinia is the Trusthouse Forte village near the attractive coastal resort of Santa Margherita di Pula. Open from May to the end of September, it is a big, lively complex, attractively set in pinewoods on the beach, and with a huge choice of sports and recreation facilities. The village, practically a resort-within-a-resort, consists of 600 bungalows, built in rustic style, and from which guests are within easy walking distance of the beach, the sports centre, the main piazza, with its boutiques and theatre, restaurants and bars.

In addition, the complex boasts a stylish 135-room hotel, the Castello, set in a secluded part of the village grounds. An imposing Conference Centre opened here recently with a main hall capable of accommodating 952 delegates seated theatre-style.

The Forte Village is a particular favourite with British visitors, and is extensively featured in travel companies' brochures.

STINTINO

The appealing fishing village of Stintino, on the northwestern corner of Sardinia near the tip of a narrow peninsula, is in the process of becoming an important resort. Much less expensive than the Costa Smeralda, the resort nevertheless has a great deal of charm, and facilities and amenities are being agreeably planned and executed. There is an excellent beach, and Stintino is a good choice for those, particularly families, looking for a beach holiday that will not cost them the earth.

CAPO CACCIA

North of Capo Caccia, with its dramatic cliffs and fascinating caves, are numerous small holiday resorts: Porto Ferro, Argentiera and Nurra, to name but three, all quite tiny and with comparatively limited facilities. They are tailor-made at present to those seeking a quieter beach resort holiday, and are happy with good but unsophisticated hotel accommodation.

Also in the northwest is a stretch of coastline between Isola Rossa and Porto di Li Francesi which has been given the name Costa Paradiso; in between are a few beaches with several hotels and numerous villas managed by individuals and private organisations.

OLBIA

Visitors to Sardinia from Britain are likely to land, either by air or by one of the most scenic routes – by boat from Civitavecchia, near Rome – at the little port of Olbia, an attractive harbour connected by a train which runs through the centre of the island to Cagliari in the south. Olbia is an ancient city and its gulf particularly scenic, with many developing resorts; Lido del Sole to the south and Lido Pittilungu to the north being among the most popular. Not far from Olbia is the Golfo degli Aranci, an attractive fishing town with some splendid beaches nearby.

TOWN AND RESORT GUIDE

Aggius

Aggius is the home of 'artistic granite' – incredible natural works of art created by the wind. The village treats its visitors with courtesy, and in turn they are rewarded with popular traditions including one of the few varieties of Sardinian song which adopts counterpoint; a sharp principal voice is accompanied by the four voices of the chorus, creating an organ-like effect. The town has a famous choir, and its second claim to fame is that it witnessed a particularly vehement feud between two families which killed 72 and left only six survivors. A major attraction is that the wine and natural 'spumante' produced in the area are of first rate quality.

ALGHERO

Alghero is a beautiful town in a beautiful setting: one of the prime holiday centres of Sardinia and a particular favourite with the British, who have been coming here for decades.

Protected by its ancient walls and towers, it lies between the sea and its fertile hinterland rich in olive trees and vines, and over the past decades its economy has been transformed from being based mainly on fishing and agriculture to becoming very much tourist-oriented. This is thanks to the beauty of the environment where the ancient part of the city, with its characteristic streets and shops, the seaside walkways, the Aragonesque Gothic churches and the Catalan tradition of the population contrast with, and complement, the attractions of the splendid beaches nearby and the holiday resorts that are also rich in items of archaeological interest, such as the Carthaginian necropolis of Anghelu Ruju, and natural beauty, including the fantastic Neptune grottos at Capo Caccia.

Alghero has the appearance of having been built for noblemen, which it was, and most of the fortifications of the old town are still intact. On the seaward side the top of the walls makes a promenade with views of the town and its gulf, while five towers remain on the landward side; the Torre dello Sperone, the southernmost, is also called the Torre di Sulis after the Sardinian revolutionary who was imprisoned there following Angioy's rebellion, while the Torre di Porta Terra marks the old main gate.

Alghero retains a marked Catalan flavour, and until recently practically everyone here spoke Catalan, though nowadays it is only the older ones that still do. The city's landmark is the 16th century cathedral on Via Manno, whose interior, unlike most churches in Sardinia, is more interesting than its plain façade, with three lofty naves separated by alternating pillars and columns, an octagonal dome, and a Baroque pulpit and altar, behind which is a 19th century monument to Maurice Duke of Savoy, a neo-classical study of women and nymphs.

Across the street from the cathedral is the Palazzo d'Albis, where Emperor Charles stayed during a visit, and nearby the Via Carlo Alberto, containing a good selection of shops. Also in the old town are the Casa Doria, a splendid 16th century palace on the Via Principe Umberto; the Municipio, on the Piazza Municipio, containing Alghero's historical archives; and two interesting churches on Via Carlo Alberto: San Michele (17th century) with a multicoloured tile dome; and the 14th century San Francisco, which has a beautiful interior. Just outside the old town, across from the Torre di Porta Terra, is a pretty park, the Giardino Pubblico.

Tourism has been an important element in Alghero's economy since the early 1960s, and the town has excellent facilities, typical restaurants, and craft shops where they make and exhibit the famous red coral found in the sea close to the town, and which makes excellent collectors' items.

EXCURSIONS

Since the success of the Costa Smeralda every strip of Sardinian coast has been given a label, and the coastal area bordering Alghero is no exception. In this case the name chosen, 'Costa del Corallo,' does have some relevance because of the local coral. North of Alghero is a huge sandy beach that runs for several kilometres, all the way to Fertilia, a town founded by Mussolini as the centre of a big agricultural reclamation area, and on the stream just before Fertilia are the remains of a Roman bridge. Beyond the town is another beach, Le Bombarde, and the Palmavera Nuraghe, then a bay with some small undeveloped beaches.

The western side of the bay is another of Sardinia's natural wonders: Capo Caccia, with its dramatic cliffs and views of Alghero and the two great rocks in the sea, Isola Piano and Isola Forada. Near the cape the cliffs are several hundred metres high, forcing the visitor to walk down 650 steps to visit the Grotta di Nettuno, but the effort is certainly worth it, since this is undoubtedly one of the most beautiful caves in the world.

In the summer there are frequent boat trips from the harbour to Capo Caccia, the Bombarde and other pleasant seaside localities.

Another interesting excursion is to the Sanctuary of Valverde. Legend says that a statue of the Madonna was mysteriously found here and when it was placed in the cathedral it also mysteriously disappeared from there, to reappear at its present location, where a chapel was subsequently built, and throughout April and May pilgrims from many parts of the island flock here to pay their respects.

North of Alghero, off the road for Porto Torres, is the great Neolithic necropolis of Angelu Ruiu, the largest in Sardinia, whose 36 *domus de janus* have interesting decorations, mostly of bulls' heads. Near the necropolis is Fertilia airport, which serves Sassari, Alghero and Porto Torres.

Regional cooking is rich: the lobsters from the Alghero sea, though expensive, are the high point of the cuisine, along with other fish and sea food specialities.

USEFUL ADDRESSES

TOURIST INFORMATION
Piazza Porta Terra 9, tel. 979054

HOTELS
Villa las Tronas, tel. 975390
Calabona, tel. 975728
Gran Catalunya, tel. 978471
La Margherita, tel. 979006
Mediterraneo, tel. 979201

RESTAURANTS
Da Torre, 4 Via Gioberti
Il Pavone, Piazza Sulis, tel. 979584 (with an attractive terrace overlooking the sea)
Corsaro, Via Columbano, tel. 978431
Diecimetri, 37 Vicola Adami, tel. 979023
La Lepanto, 135 Via Carlo Alberto, tel. 979159
Da Pietro, 20 Via Machin, tel. 979645

TRAVEL AGENCIES
Agenzie Maritime Sarde, Corso V. Emanuele 7, tel. 979005
Agritours, Via U. Foscolo
Cunedda Viaggi, Via Lamarmora 34, tel. 977879
Island Tours, Via Kennedy 7/c
Magic Tours, Piazza Sulis 14, tel. 979539
Smeral Tours, Via Sulis 7, tel. 979577

CAR HIRE
Acanfora, Aeroporto Fertilia, tel. 935060
Adama, Via Kennedy 96, tel. 976797
Algtours, Piazza Sulis, tel. 970539
Autonoleggio Italia, Aeroporto Fertilia, tel. 977879
Autonoleggio Magic Tours, Piazza Sulis 7, tel. 976439
Cadoni, Via Rossini 16, tel. 976146
Demontis Autonoleggio, Aeroporto Fertilia, tel. 935064
Hertz Italiana, Aeroporto Fertilia, tel. 935054
Maggiore Autoservizi, Aeroporto Fertilia, tel. 935045; Piazza
Sulis 1, tel. 979375
Nieddu, Via S. Satta 46, tel. 951505
Nolauto Sarda, Aeroporto Fertilia, tel. 935032
Nurra, Via De Gasperi, tel. 979515
Salaris, Via V. Veneto 11 tel. 979221

AUTOMOBILE CLUB
Via Mazzini, tel. 979659

ALITALIA
Agenzia Oliva, Corso V. Emanuele 11, tel. 979063

AIR TERMINAL
Corso V. Emanuele 11

Arbatax

The little town of Arbatax, noted for its red cliffs and pink sand beaches, overlooks the sea at the tip of a short peninsula of Capo Bellavista, and has a good harbour for commercial and tourist craft, which is one reason for its development into a small holiday resort. Its name suggests an exotic origin and recalls the times of the Saracen raids in the Mediterranean. Gastronomic tradition here is excellent, with the emphasis on the basic ingredients supplied by the fishing boats that ply the harbour.

Granite houses stretch along the headland, and most of the inhabitants are connected with fishing, the port and its ferry service to Olbia and Genoa, or with the railway, this being the end of the line from Cagliari on this side of the island.

Nearby are some interesting towers, built by the Spaniards against African pirates, and later converted into customs look-out posts; and the mountain resort of Lanusei, the largest town of a small region called the Ogliastro.

USEFUL ADDRESSES

HOTELS
Cala Moresca, tel. 667366
Villagio Saraceno, tel. 667318 (excellent sports facilities)
La Bitta, tel. 667080
Telis, tel. 667081

TRAVEL AGENCY
Toratour, Via Lungomore 38, tel. 667268

Ardara

An important centre in the Middle Ages, almost rivalling Sassari, Ardara was the old capital of the Giudicato region before the Spanish occupation. It is worth visiting if only for its 12th century church of Santa Maria del Regno, built of dark basalt; in pure Romanesque style, it was to become a model for other, later churches in Sardinia. Inside, the nave and two side aisles are divided by massive columns, and contain some interesting frescoes which, alas, are in a poor condition. The beautiful 15th century altarpiece contains 31 individual panels painted by Martin Torner and Giovani Ruiu. The church was intended to be the chapel of the nearby 12th century castle, and was built by a Sard heroine who led troops to defeat the usurper of the Giudice of Gallura whom she imprisoned in her castle. The castle was captured from the Dorias by the Aragonese in 1335 and 20 years later was sold to the Giudice of Arborea, and subsequently claimed by the Kings of Aragon, before falling into decay in the 15th century.

Nearby
The country church of Saint Antiocco di Bisarcio is older than Santa Maria de Regno but has been altered several times over the

centuries. It was built in 1150–90 as a cathedral for the whole of Logudoro, on the site of an earlier church, dating from 1090, which had burnt down. Of particular interest are some beautiful frescoes dating from the early 13th century and which, despite Byzantine influence, are attributed to an unknown Pisan artist.

Aritzo

Once a village with a purely mountain economy, Aritzo is now making a name for itself as a holiday resort, thanks to the position of the town, high on the edge of the Gennargentu massif. The extension of the road to Arcu Guddetorgiu, which continues to Arcu Tascusi, makes for easy access to the highest vantage points in Sardinia. The village's late Gothic 16th century parish church has a fine passion cross by a silversmith from Cagliari, dating from the 14th century.

Aritzo remains the chestnut 'capital' of the island, and a grand fair is held every year to celebrate the distinction.

USEFUL ADDRESSES

HOTELS
Sa Muvara, Via Kennedy, tel. 629336
Castello, Via Umberto 169, tel. 629266
La Capannina, Via A. Maxia 36, tel. 629121
Moderno, Via Kennedy 6, tel. 629229
Park Hotel, Via A. Maxia, tel. 629201

Arzachena

Originally no more than a peasant village in the mountains to the west of the Costa Smeralda, Arzachena has grown into a large settlement with no particular features to interest the holidaymaker of its own, but plenty in the immediate neighbourhood, especially the unusual rock tombs. People of the Arzachena culture, from

3,000 BC onwards, lived in hollows in the granite rocks, which are typical of the area, and the technique of using stone walls to protect natural rock holes from wind and weather is still employed by shepherds of the Gallura. The tombs themselves, which differ from the usual burial chambers of the period, are square box graves with a round covering hill and upright granite rocks; they are concentrated on the heights in the north east of the area, with the finest of them to be seem at Li Muri.

Baia Sardinia

Life in this little resort, which lies on the edge of the Costa Smeralda, about five miles from Porto Cervo, revolves round a wide, curving beach, lapped by incredibly clear water – wonderful for swimming and windsurfing, and one of the most attractive beaches on the island.

From the promenade along the beach the village rises up the gentle slope around the bay and though small, comprising mainly of villas with a handful of hotels, the resort provides for most needs, with several bars and restaurants, including one on the beach. Around the headland there are other beautiful sandy beaches, including the lovely bays of Tre Monti and Golfo degli Ulivi. A new supermarket has opened to serve these areas, and there is a tennis club in the village, while windsurfing is available on the main beach.

USEFUL ADDRESSES

HOTELS
La Bisaccia, tel. 99002
Club Hotel, tel. 99006 (very comfortable, with attractive terraces)
Smeraldo Beach, tel. 99046
Mon Repos Hermitage, tel. 99011
Residence Park, tel. 99016
Cormorano, tel. 90020
Delle Vigne, tel. 99157
Le Tre Botti, tel. 99150
Villa Gemella, tel. 99303

RESTAURANT
Le Tre Botti, located at Lisoia di Vacca turn-off, tel. 99150

TRAVEL AGENCIES
Rena Bianca Tours, Centro Comm. Rena Bianca
Smeral Tours, Piazzetta, tel. 789/99152
Unimare, Piazzetta Centrale, tel. 0789/99144

Bari Sardo

In recent years this little centre has been considerably developed
for holiday and residential purposes. This is not only because of its
beaches, such as that at Torre di Bari, just 5 km away, which is
pleasant with good sand and shady woods, and takes its name from
a fine watch-tower that once stood guard against Saracen invaders,
but because it sits in a nest of nuraghi interspersed with vineyards
and almond groves. There are hotels and restaurants in the village
and at Torre di Bari, while the church in Bari Sardo contains an
interesting copy of Raphael's *Holy Family* by the Sard painter
Antioco Mainas.

USEFUL ADDRESSES

HOTELS
Il Cantuccio, Via Mare, tel. 29653
Nuraghe Kortiakas, tel. 29658
La Torre, tel. 29577

Barumini

The little farming community of Barumini acquired extraordinary
importance in archaeological history with the excavation, in the
1950s, of the biggest Nuraghic settlement in Sardinia, 'Su Nuraxi'.
The development was unknown until 1899 when a mudslide
uncovered it, and though its origins are uncertain it is thought that,

because wood was used in its construction it represented not simply a village but a palace or capital, or perhaps a trading centre for the Sards and their Greek, Punic and Roman enemies. The collection of smaller towers and odd-shaped chambers, built of the same enormous stones as the castle and connected by narrow, winding alleys, evoke the Nuraghic civilisation more clearly, perhaps, than any other site on the island. Especially interesting are the two well-carved circular fountains, while in the castle itself there is a small central courtyard and a network of stairways and passages.

In the period between 2,000 and 500 BC a series of additions was made so that a fairly large village grew up around the original tall tower, creating a formidable fortified settlement. The military architecture and the civil and domestic remains in the settlement bear witness to the development and decline of Nuraghic civilisation.

Four mighty towers were placed at the four points of the compass against the original tower, surrounded by an enormous wall forming an interior courtyard in which there is a well: dug out of the rock with a depth of over 15 metres, the bottom still contains water.

About the 6th century BC a fortified outer curtain was built with polygonal walls topped by combat towers. Between the great central structure and the outer curtain, and also on the outside of the latter, are the well-preserved traces of dwellings, bakeries, and large circular huts for civic purposes showing traces of fires and the addition of building techniques applied by the victors, all of which testify to the intense military, civil and political life in Sardinia at the time of the nuraghe.

Refreshments are available in the vicinity of the archaeological site, and in the village itself there is a simple inn.

From the top of the castle there is an excellent view of another castle, the 12th century Las Plassas, at the summit of a small hill, visible for a considerable distance in all directions.

USEFUL ADDRESSES

HOTELS
S. Lucia, tel. 9368064
Su Nuraxi, tel. 9368006

Bonorva

This important town, which is known as the home of the purest language of the Logudoro, possesses fine examples of typical minor architecture. Craft production flourishes, especially carpets and tapestries, many of which are on show, and on sale, at the ISOLA Pilot Centre. But Bonorva is important, too, because it is an excellent base for fascinating excursions to nearby archaeological sites: on the plateau of Su Monte, for example, there are large megalithic enclosures, 'giants' tombs', remains of Roman roads, and the little village of Rebeccu with a sacred fountain.

Also within reach are the so-called *Grottos of Sant'Andrea Priu*, great stone burial chambers, known as *domus de janas* (houses of the fairies), and dating from about 2000 BC. Dug out of the rock, they are in places quite spacious and intercommunicating, and the site is made all the more mysterious and fascinating by the presence of solar symbols, little ritual niches and labyrinthine chambers. An enormous statue of a bull, made out of a single block of stone, stands guard over the outside of the rocky formation that houses the group of 20 tombs, adding to the magic spell of the place.

Also close by is the 'Nuraghe Palace' of Santu Antine which, along with the Nuraghic settlement at Barumini, is the most remarkable and mighty nuraghe in Sardinia. On the outside, the remains of Carthaginian and Roman buildings indicate that the site was used at a more recent period.

USEFUL ADDRESS

TOURIST INFORMATION
9 Corse Umberto

Bosa

Situated at the mouth of the river Temo, which at this point is navigable for a few kilometres, Bosa is a charming little town of ancient Carthaginian origin. In addition to the fine, well-ordered streets and squares of the modern centre, it has an interesting old quarter up against the hill, dominated by the half-ruined castle of Serravalle, built by the Pisans in the 12th century, with particularly well-preserved walls. The walk to the castle from the Piazza del Carmine up a steep slope is quite delightful, and affords good views of some of Bosa's many ancient houses, some as old as the castle itself, with double doors opening on to stone-flagged entrance halls.

Bosa's San Pietro cathedral is the oldest Romanesque church in Sardinia. Built using ancient Roman materials in 1073 by Lombard workmen under Bishop Costantino de Castro, it has an interesting frieze of animal motifs added by the Cistercian monks of S. Maria di Garavata, Bosa.

Numerous narrow alleyways lead off the Corso, with first-floor rooms built across to act as a link, while the quayside, lined with palms, is attractive and generally very lively.

Tourism has grown considerably in recent years, with visitors drawn not only by the attractions of the town itself, but also the beach at the fast-growing nearby resort of Bosa Marina, an old port with a 17th century watch tower. A small island, Isola Rossa, is joined to the port by a causeway.

Bosa is a centre for the production of olive oil and wines (its 'malvasia' is famous), and is also well known for lace, boasting several craftshops where fine lace articles are still produced. The Bosa cuisine is rich in dishes using the products of the sea, with lobsters and fish soup being the favourite dishes, though the products of animal breeding are certainly not lacking.

Just 2 km out of the town is the interesting church of San Pietro Extramuros, dating back to the 11th century, one of Sardinia's earliest and best Romanesque churches.

USEFUL ADDRESSES

TOURIST INFORMATION
Via Ciusa

HOTELS
Al Gabbiano, Viale Mediterraneo, tel. 36123
Turas, tel. 33473
Bassu, Via G. Deledda 15, tel. 33456
Miramere, Via Colombo, tel. 33400
Pirino, Via Colombo 13, tel. 33586

Buddusò

A large centre with pleasant stone buildings and stone-paved streets, Buddusò is not generally on most visitors' itineraries, though it has a well-earned reputation for hospitality, with its austere granite façades hiding warm welcomes. As well as granite and cork, the town is renowed for the skill with which its craftsmen continue to build wooden chests in the traditional manner. The chests, opening at the top, were in practice the only piece of furniture of any real value in the old houses of Sardinia. Generally made of chestnut wood, but sometimes with harder material, they have two plain sides while the fronts are finely carved with traditional floral designs, or with designs representing the sun or stylised bird shapes; sometimes the two front feet are carved in the shape of animal heads or highly stylised lion's paws, and the wood was left either in its natural state, or painted with lamb's blood. The chests have now become fashionable items of furniture, and may be bought directly from the craftsmen who make them.

USEFUL ADDRESS

HOTEL
La Madonnina, tel. 714645

Busachi

This large village stretches over a length of several kilometres along a principal road, giving it the distinction of being the longest village in Sardinia. Most of its buildings are still constructed of stone, with tiny doors and windows surrounded by brightly coloured or white cornices. Elderly residents continue to wear ancient costumes and pursue traditional activities, such as tending their vegetable gardens or spinning wool. The young people revive the old traditions on feast days, adopting authentic costumes and dancing in the village square or the church square.

Visitors can buy unusual souvenirs; the interesting church has a remarkably high bell-tower; and there are delightful views of the surrounding countryside.

USEFUL ADDRESS

TOURIST INFORMATION
Via Brigata Sassari, 159

CAGLIARI

The administrative capital of Sardinia and main port of the island, Cagliari has been inhabited ever since prehistoric times, as can be seen from the remains of lake-dwellings found in the nearby lagoons. The urban network of the town displays various elements that bear witness to the numerous influences that have moulded its history: Carthaginian burial grounds, Roman remains (amphitheatre, Villa di Tigellio, Grotta della Vipera), Pisan walls and towers (Elephant Tower, Tower of San Pancrazio), Aragonese and Spanish ramparts, Piedmontese fortifications in the old district of Castello, interesting churches such as the early Christian basilica of San Saturno, and the church of San Domenico, with its magnificent cloister.

Cagliari offers a great variety of entertainments, art exhibitions and all kinds of sports facilities, and is well equipped, too, as a holiday resort, with the immediate vicinity (Lagoons of Molentargius and Santa Gilla) offering fine scenery much appreciated by nature lovers and bird-watchers, as indeed does the Golfo degli Angeli (Gulf of the Angels) lying to the north.

The town is tailor-made for sightseers, and there are few more pleasant activities than taking a leisurely stroll during the morning, with a drink at a comfortable pavement café in the Via Roma to watch the comings and goings at the port.

Flights of flamingoes, cormorants, ducks and herons are an everyday sight, as they pass over the town moving from one lagoon to the other, and at sunset an extraordinary pink light spreads over the ancient walls and ramparts.

Rome left her mark in Cagliari's grandiose amphitheatre, with its auditorium carved out of the rock, the Villa di Tigellio, and the Grotta della Vipera; Pisa left the splendid 13th century towers known as the Elephant Tower and the Tower of San Pancrazio;

while the Aragonese and the Spaniards gave the town its walls and ramparts and fine buildings distinguished by wrought-iron balconies.

Of particular interest to the visitor is the old part of Cagliari. This is a tourist 'must', for while the newer districts, built after the war, give Cagliari the appearance of a modern town, the old town has managed to retain the discreet charm of its original character and from the airy terraces of the district of Castello, once the fortifications of the Pisan and Aragonese overlords, there are wonderful views.

Reached through ancient medieval gates, Castello maintains the appearance of an old fortified town almost cut off from the rest, with its ramparts, its narrow streets, and two powerful medieval towers; and one of the most spectacular means of approaching the Castello district is by the flight of steps from the Piazza Costituzione through an elegant arch.

Also of particular interest to the visitor is Cagliari's cathedral which dominates the Piazza Palazzo. The church was originally built between 1257 and 1312 in Romanesque style and got its Baroque interior from Domenico Spotorno in the 17th century. This was changed once more, in 1933, by the architect Giarrizzo who added neo-Pisan touches, and is very ornate, with rounded arches and square pillars separating the three naves, and a floor of black, white and mottled pink marble. In one of the Baroque side chapels is a 14th century gold-painted wooden Madonna and child, a silver tabernacle on the altar dating from 1610, and the mausoleum of Martin II of Aragon, by the 17th century Genoese sculpter Giulio Aprile; it is in the same mottled marble as the floor, with life-sized angels and warriors fronted by a simple tomb.

By far the most stunning and unusual part of the cathedral is the sanctuary reached through a door on the altar steps, one part of which is dedicated to the 17th century Bishop Esquivel who built it 300 years after the foundation of the cathedral itself. A second chapel is the mausoleum, sculpted by Andrea Galassi of Marie Josephine Louise, wife of Louis XVIII of France, who died in exile in 1810 at Harwell in Buckinghamshire, and at whose own request, as the daughter of the King of Sardinia, her body was brought to Cagliari a year after her death.

Perhaps the most interesting aspects of the sanctuary, however, is not these tombs but the walls, hewn out of rock and into which 17th century Sicilian artists carved a vast array of niches with bas-reliefs of all the Sardinian saints. Their ashes were said to have been found beneath the ruins of the church of San Saturnino in 1617.

Not far from the cathedral is the university, an original 18th century building designed by Captain Belgromo di Famolasio and still in use. Beyond it is the first of the two famous towers, the Tower of the Elephant, built in 1307 during Pisan domination by the architect Giovanni Capula, and which derives its names from a statue of an elephant set on a high ledge. It is a massive medieval construction with three sides enclosed and the fourth, towards the city, left open. The tower and its brother on the opposite end of the ramparts – San Pancrazio, in Piazza Independenza – were the two most important defensive points of the castle of Cagliari.

The cathedral is flanked by the Governor's Palace, built in 1769 and formerly the royal palace of the House of Savoy, containing valuable frescoes by Domenico Bruschi as well as ornate rooms; and by the imposing Archbishop's Palace, designed by the same architect; while on the opposite corner of the piazza is the 17th century Music Conservatory.

In the Piazza Indipendenza is the National Archaeological Museum, the nucleus of which was the private collection of Carol Felice who, in 1806, give it to the university, since when it has been greatly expanded. Of the Nuraghic items, the most spectacular are contained in several showcases: the famous bronze statuettes, varying in height from four inches to about a foot and a half. Other important finds from this age come from Tharros, a ruined Roman town, with exhibits including funeral stones, coffins, tombs with paintings, a sacrificial altar, and a sacred lion.

The display of Roman jewellery is substantial, and includes engraved gold panels no bigger than postcards, one with writing found at Nora and the other a frieze of human figures, with animal heads. The glassware, mainly from Tharros, Karalis (the Roman name for Cagliari) and Cornus, is in the form of vases, and there is also an extensive coin collection. Above the museum is an art gallery showing the development of painting in Sardinia from the 14th to the 17th centuries.

Other places of interest in Cagliari include the remains of the home in Via Tigellio of Tigellius, a Sardinian poet and singer much favoured by the Roman emperor Augustus as well as by Caius Caesar and Cleopatra. Then there is the Grotto of the Viper, the tomb of an exiled Roman pair and so called because above the portal are sculptured two serpents; the construction is as high as a three-storey house, and to the side of the tombs a flight of steps leads up to the Punic necropolis on the top of the hill that was the cemetery of ancient Karalis.

Finally there is the Roman amphitheatre, built about the same time as the Colosseum in Rome, and almost completely carved out of rock. Close by are the Botanical gardens.

FESTIVAL

The Sant'Efisio Festival held on 1 May each year is colourful and lively, with costumes and performers from all over the island. The highlight is a pilgrimage to the saint's shrine at Nora, with the saint's image carried on an elaborate float and decorated ox-carts.

St Efisio is credited with removing the plague from Cagliari in 1656, from which time the town authorities instituted a festival in thanksgiving to him. He is also said to be responsible for other remarkable feats, including the withdrawal of a French invasion in 1793 when he produced such a storm that the enemy fleet was forced to retreat. Today's ceremonies are a marvellous mixture of folklore and religion, spectacle and fun.

EXCURSIONS

Cagliari is a good centre for some interesting excursions. Within easy reach is Dolianova, which has an interesting 12th century Romanesque church; Senorbi, the main centre of the Trexnta area, with an interesting parish church; and Suelli, which also has a fine church, San Giorgio, with a late Gothic bell-tower and some excellent statues in polychrome wood.

Many visitors choosing Cagliari as a base also pay a visit to the well and temple of Santa Vittoria, one of the most impressive reminders of the cult of the waters practised by the ancient people of the Nuraghi. Around the holy well stand various buildings both religious and civic, which were used for worship or as meeting places for non-religious and even commercial purposes.

Excursions are also popular to Barumini, with its extraordinary fortress of 'Su Nuraxi,' to Villanovaforru, just outside which a Nuraghic settlement has been discovered fairly recently; the pleasant little agricultural town of Sanluri; and to the Carthaginian-Roman temple at Antas, whose fine Ionic columns are topped by an interesting entablature with the remains of Roman inscriptions.

USEFUL ADDRESSES

TOURIST INFORMATION
Piazza Deffenu 9, tel. 663207/654811; and Via Mameli 97,
 tel. 664195

HOTELS
Mediterraneo, Lungomare Colombo 46, tel. 301271
Moderno, Via Roma 159, tel. 653971
Al Solemar, Viale Diaz, tel. 301360
Italia, Via Sardegna, tel. 655772

RESTAURANTS
Dal Corsaro, Viale Regina Margherita 28, tel. 664318
Al Golfo, at Hotel Mediterraneo, Lungomare Colombo,
 tel. 301271
Ottagono, Viale Poetto, tel. 372879
Buongustaio, Via Concezione 7, tel. 668124
Italia, Via Sardegna 30, tel. 657987
Rosetta, Via Sardegna 44, tel. 663131

BRITISH CONSULATE
Via S. Lucifero, tel. 662755

CAR HIRE
Avis, Via Sonnino 87, tel. 668128
Europcar, Aeroporto Elmas, tel. 240126
Hertz, Piazza Matteotti 8, tel. 663457/668105; Aeroporto Elmas,
 tel. 240037

TRAVEL AGENCIES
Acentro Div. Turismo, Via Sonnino 57, tel. 651618
Airmar, Via Tola 2, tel. 490311
Antalya, Piazza Yenne 40, tel. 668731
Asatur, Via Dante 122, tel. 43273
Cosmorama, Piazza Repubblica 8, tel. 497872
Feeling, Via Campania 45, tel. 291255
Grimmtour, Via Einaudi 10, tel. 664037
Il Planisfero, Viale Bonaria 118
Karalis, Via della Pineta 199, tel. 306991
Nautilus, Via Castiglione 31, tel. 40309
Passport, Via Amat 1, tel. 304980

President, Via Sonnino 95, tel. 664940
Sardamondial, Viale Regina Margherita 8, tel. 668094
Sardivet, Viale S. Avendrace 191, tel. 288978
Sartourist, Piazza Deffenu 14, tel. 652971
Starplay, Via dei Mille 8, tel. 668734
Viaggi Orru, Via Roma 95, tel. 657954
World Travel Jet, Via Alghero 48, tel. 653256
Zucca Paola, Via Campidano 3, tel. 654668

AIR TERMINAL
Piazza Matteotti

Cala Gonone

Cala Gonone, an attractive little seaside resort with a harbour,
numerous hotels, restaurants and craft shops, lures visitors year
round, not only by its climate and the many national and
international cultural events held here, but because this is the
departure point for boat trips to the nearby grotto of Blue Marino,
part of the Karst system of the massif of Supramonte. The small
opening on the seaward side leads the way into miles of natural
treasures, inhabited by a few families of monkseals, the last
specimen of fauna from the far-off times when glaciers reached the
Mediterranean. To make a trip to the grotto you need half a day,
and good weather for the crossing. A tour of the grotto is a
fascinating experience, and a pleasant one since it is dry and not
slippery or damp like many caves; it is also hot inside, instead of
the clamminess evident in many caves. There are various caves
with lacy stalactites in pinks, whites, creams and browns, while the
species of seal said to live here is called Monachus Albiventer,
surviving from the Ice Age.
   Numerous hotels and restaurants, some of them open
year-round, together with an excellent selection of villas, many for
rent, make Cala Gonone one of Sardinia's most attractive holiday
resorts.

Nearby
Santa Maria Navarrese, with a picturesque tower, beach and 11th
century church built by the daughter of the King of Navarre.

139

USEFUL ADDRESSES

HOTELS
Mastino 'Dello Grazie', tel. 93150
Costa Dorada, tel. 93333
Villaggio Palmasera, tel. 93191
Nuttuno, tel. 93310
La Favorita, tel. 93169
La Playa, tel. 93106
Miramare, tel. 93140
L'Oasis, tel. 791117
Blue Marino, tel. 93130

Capo Boi

Capo Boi, located quite close to Villasimius, is an attractive little resort that is being increasingly featured in tour operators' programmes thanks to its pleasant beach, while nearby is another little resort, Solanus, also with a pretty beach and with the bonus of a sentinel tower on a headland.

USEFUL ADDRESS

HOTEL
Capo Boi, tel. 791515 (a very smart beach hotel with pool, set in attractive wooded grounds)

CAPRERA ISLAND

I offer you hunger, thirst, forced marches, battles and death. Anyone who loves his country, follow me.

GIUSEPPE GARIBALDI

Caprera island is a barren, rocky place linked to the island of La Maddalena by a causeway, and is included in many visitors' itineraries largely because of its associations with Giuseppe Garibaldi, Italy's great 19th century hero who became owner of Caprera and for nearly 30 years regarded it as his home and refuge until his death in June 1882. Garibaldi's house on Caprera, the Casa Bianca, is now a national museum, its garden laid out approximately as it was in Garibaldi's day with, in the centre of the courtyard, an enormous tree he planted to celebrate the birth of his daughter, Clelia, in 1867. The last of his children to survive, she died aged 92 on 2 February 1959, and is buried in the family cemetery a short distance from the house.

Not far from Garibaldi's home and garden is a Club Med. complex, whose round thatched-roof rondavels have bamboo walls and a door, but no windows; it is a remote and peaceful setting.

Castelsardo

A fortified town founded by the Genoese in the 12th century, Castelsardo is set on a promontory overlooking vast panoramas . . . the Gulf of Asinara to the west and the Gallura mountain peaks to the east. The ancient town still preserves the structures of military defence, while the more modern buildings spread out towards the hinterland.

Castelsardo has seen rapid growth in its tourist industry, and is today a popular holiday resort, thanks to its small but well equipped port. The town's 'ateliers' are well known for the

141

production of typical baskets made from the leaves of miniature palm trees woven together, and visitors can also find numerous other types of attractive Sardinian craftsmanship.

The town preserves the ancient tradition of Easter Week during which all the ceremonies are of medieval origin and are thus older than the Spanish rites adopted in the rest of Sardinia. Called 'Lunissanti,' these ceremonies are accompanied by Gregorian chant and candlelight processions. Castelsardo's cathedral, whose construction was begun in the 16th century during the late Gothic period, is characteristic of Sardinia, being set on the cliff edge, and is notable for its 18th century carved wooden altars and choir stalls and for a gilt and wood pulpit covered with cherubs. But its masterpiece is a madonna and child with angels playing music, painted by an unknown artist.

Nearby
The elephant of Castelsardo, an eroded tachylite rock, is a famous feature. However, it is not the shape that makes it important historically, but the little-known domus de janas concealed inside it.

USEFUL ADDRESSES

TOURIST INFORMATION
Via Bastione 2

HOTELS
Castello, tel. 470062
Hotel Villagio Pedra Ladda, tel. 470383
Riviera, tel. 470143
Baja Ostina, tel. 470223, 3 km away at Cala Ostina
S'Istaffa, tel. 470010, 4 km away at Lu Bagnu

RESTAURANTS
La Guardiola, Piazza del Bastione, tel. 470428
Riviera-Da Fofò, Via Roma 105, tel. 470143
Sa Ferula, at Lu Bagnu, tel. 474049

TRAVEL AGENCIES
Sea Gull Travel, Via Veneto 5, tel. 470495

COSTA SMERALDA

Some of the finest beaches in Sardinia are to be found on the Costa Smeralda, a breathtaking stretch of coastline originally conceived for the exclusive international 'jet set', and now a flourishing area renowned for its yacht club and marina and for its outstanding sporting facilities and excellent hotels. The architectural theme is to make villas, shops and hotels look as if they have grown out of their surroundings, and though some may complain that the end result is artificial, the overall effect is discreet and luxurious and forms an exclusive international playground.

The project, comprising several hundred acres, is fairly recent. In the 1960's the Aga Khan and a group of friends decided to buy land in what was then an almost depopulated area. First they built their own homes, then formed a consortium giving them absolute control over who buys land, what may be built, and where.

In practical terms this means that all telephone and electricity cables are carried underground, that no sewage is allowed to flow into the sea, and that the owner with 2,400 square metres can use only 200 of these for his house: in other words, a ratio of about 10% building to 90% land. Conservation is taken seriously, the rocks, plants, shrubs and so on being carefully removed from the site before building starts and replanted at its conclusion, which is one reason why gardens look so well established and in keeping with the surroundings.

Executives of the Costa Smeralda claim that it is not only the international jet set who benefit from the development of the region but the Sards themselves, many of whom are returning to Gallura having emigrated from what was once the poorest region in the island.

The heart of the Costa Smeralda is Porto Cervo, an intriguing maze of colour-washed houses where the selection of bars, shops

143

and restaurants includes some tempting boutiques. The old harbour and a superb, recently extended marina, provide mooring for fabulous yachts.

From the piazza in Porto Cervo a little wooden bridge separates the inner canal moorings, used mainly by day boats, from the main yacht anchorages, and a path leads to the Cervo Tennis Club whose unostentatious building and facilities, on payment of daily, weekly or monthly fees, include indoor and outdoor pools, upstairs lounge and restaurant: all handy amenities for villa owners.

Up the hill from Porto Cervo stretches the Sa Conca arcade designed by Michel Busiri Vici of Rome, who was also the architect of an hotel and the Stella Maris church, built in 1968. The church is very small, with graceful rounded arches, a green granite floor and fascinating lights like delicate steel cones, and its main attraction is El Greco's masterpiece 'Mater Dolorosa,' donated in 1969 by Baroness Bentinck when her husband was Dutch Ambassador in Paris.

Along the deeply indented coastline a series of soft, sandy beaches retain their unspoiled beauty, although a few exclusive hotels and some attractively designed villas have grown up near them to cater for the growing numbers of holidaymakers attracted to the area.

Another bonus for visitors, especially the golfing fraternity, is the superbly landscaped Pevero Golf Course which enjoys some of the loveliest views in the Mediterranean from its immaculate greens. The 72 par course was designed by Robert Trent Jones to test the best professionals, and is used as a championship course on the international circuit, while the Club House has a relaxing bar, a noted restaurant and a swimming pool.

Nearby
Not far from Porto Cervo is Cala di Volpe, the Bay of Foxes, with several tiny islands off-shore. An hotel of the same name is a surrealistic castle-style structure with rough walls.

USEFUL ADDRESSES

HOTELS
Cala di Volpe, tel. 96083 (Secluded and exclusive, with attractive architecture and furnishings)
Pitrizza, tel. 92000 (Very private and select on secluded bay)

Romazzino, large and comfortable, tel. 96020
Balocco, at Liscia di Vacca, tel. 92197 (Excellent views)
Le Ginestre, near Porto Cervo, tel. 92030
Cervo, at Porto Cervo, tel. 92003 (At the centre of things with the
    atmosphere of an exclusive but informal club)
Cervo Tennis Club, tel. 92244
Capriccioli, tel. 96004

Desulo

Desulo is a typical Sardinian mountain village and the closest to the
peaks of Bruncu Spina and La Marmora, the highest points of the
island. Clinging to the west face of a deep gorge and arranged in a
series of layers, creating an interplay of perspective, the village is
famed throughout Sardinia for the traditional female costumes of
red woollen fabric with characteristic embroidered caps, found in
most parts of the island because the shepherds from Desulo set up
'colonies' more or less everywhere. It is also well known for carved
wooden utensils and implements, such as spoons and dishes.

Friendly, hospitable and enterprising, the people of Desulo are
renowned for their longevity which they attribute to their wine,
and also for their hospitality, so that the visitor is generally
assured of a pleasant stay in dramatic mountain surroundings. The
village boasts restaurants and hotels, while the local cuisine is
distinguished by tasty hams and sausages, delicious cheeses, and
boiled mutton.

USEFUL ADDRESSES

HOTELS
Gennargentu, tel. 61270
Lamarmora, tel. 66126

Dorgali

This characteristic centre is noted for the production of a famous wine known as 'canonau' and for its coloured pottery. Craft production has risen to an almost industrial level, with splendid tapestries, carpets, leather and metal work, as well as the traditional ceramics which have graduated from the role of everyday household items to become decorative ornaments and furnishings. The town, originally a Saracen settlement, boasts a selection of hotels and restaurants, while the attractive little beach resort of Cala Gonone is only 9 km away. Also nearby, at Serra Orrios, is the largest and best preserved Nuraghic village in the island, on the shores of a lake created from the damming of the River Cedrino. Excavations have revealed 70 or more round-hut dwellings, a common well and a stone central hearth called Domu de su Fumu.

There is also a very strange retreat at Monte Tiscali, believed to have been occupied during the Roman period by rebellious Sards, who felt safe in their cave hideaway.

USEFUL ADDRESSES

HOTELS
Su Babbu Mannu, tel. 95116
Il Querceto, tel. 96509

TRAVEL AGENCY
Falctour, Via Lamarmora 163, tel. 95170

Fonni

Although it is on the road to becoming an important tourist centre with the inauguration of hotels and a ski slope, the mountain village of Fonni remains closely tied to its traditional economy based on sheep and cattle rearing. Old customs live on, especially the traditional festivities connected with pastoral activities. Of particular interest is the Sanctuary of the Virgin of Martyrs where, on the Sunday after Pentecost, there is a spring festival that attracts pilgrims from throughout the surrounding area. The Sporting Club Hotel is a skiing centre in winter – the slopes of Bruncu Spina are quite close – while in summer it caters for those who enjoy horse riding, tennis and swimming. All year round the hotel takes guests on photographic safaris to see the protected moufflon that survive up here – or, at least, to try to catch a glimpse of them. Fonni is also a good starting point for excursions and ascents to the Punta Lamarmora and the other peaks of the Gennargentu.

USEFUL ADDRESSES

HOTELS
Cualbu, tel. 57054
Sporting Club, at Monte Spada, tel. 57154 (Lovely location above
    the town, with impressive views; serves authentic Sardinian
    cuisine)

Golfo Degli Aranci

Situated on the northern inlet of the Bay of Olbia, this attractive small resort offers holidaymakers a rewarding venue for a relaxing, essentially beach-type holiday. The village contains a small number of shops and coffee bars as an alternative to several well-appointed hotels, and it is to here that many ferries operate from mainland Italy, making the harbour area particularly lively.

USEFUL ADDRESSES

HOTELS
Baia Caddinas, tel. 46898 (Attractively furnished bungalows,
    together with swimming pool)
Gabbiano Azzurro, tel. 46929 (Directly on the beach, just outside
    town)
Castello, tel. 46073
Margherita. tel. 46906
King's, tel. 46075

Iglesias

Of Pisan origin, but known previously by the Romans who exploited the rich mineral resources of the area, Iglesias preserves its original character as a lively centre with a Tuscan flavour, and is an extremely pleasant place despite the fact it has always been a mining town.

It boasts an interesting range of ancient monuments . . . old city walls, Aragonese castle, 13th century cathedral, church of Santa Chiara, and monumental church of Our Lady of Valverde. All the churches were built in their original form by Pisan architects and later rebuilt in the Aragonese Gothic style.

Iglesias is also noted for its interesting Holy Week rites, which go back to the times of the Spanish influence, while peasant tradition and the world of farming and stock breeding have always lived side by side, which can be seen in the wide range of traditional products (bread, cheese and ham, etc) to be found in so many of the town's shops and restaurants.

The town has an interesting mineralogical museum housed in the Technical Institute, and there are hotels and restaurants.

The centre of Iglesias is the Piazza Quintino Sella, named after the famous vintner, whose label 'Sella and Mosca' is bottled in Alghero. Via Matteotti, leading from the piazza, is the main shopping street.

Nearby
One of the most unusual and little-known archaeological sites in Sardinia, the Tempio di Antas, is easily reached from Iglesias. Originally a Nuraghic temple, it was subsequently taken over by the Phoenicians, while under Roman rule the mixed population constructed their own version of a Classical temple with odd Ionic-style columns. The basic structure is well preserved, with floors, rooms and other areas intended for use by the priests and the faithful.

East of Iglesias is another mining town, Domusnovas, on the outskirts of which is the famous Grotta di San Giovanni, a natural tunnel in the rock.

USEFUL ADDRESSES

TOURIST INFORMATION
Piazza Municipio

HOTELS
Artu, tel. 22492
Pan di Zucchero, tel. 47114

TRAVEL AGENCY
Plaisant, Piazza Sella 4, tel. 22257

Ittireddu

The little town of Ittireddu is of considerable importance because
of its archaeological museum which is excellently arranged and
includes numerous findings, photographs, explanatory panels and
reconstructions concerning the rich historical and archaeological
heritage of the region of Montecauto. This area also includes the
necropolis sites at Monte Ruju, Monte Pira, Partulesi and Monte
Nieddu, as well as a great many nuraghi, holy wells such as the one
at Funtana 'e Baule, and other interesting monuments including
some from the Roman and medieval periods.

Laconi

An attractive village among the hills, Laconi is a popular spot for
exursions and summer and winter holidays, and also attracts a
number of pilgrims, following the beatification of Fra Ignazio of
Laconi. Among the village's most attractive features is its park,
where generations of the Aymerich family have planted and
tended trees from almost every part of the temperate hemisphere,
giving rise to a kind of growing museum. The park, open to the
public, is impressive in its own right, but its attractions are
enhanced by a sparkling waterfall and the well-preserved remains
of a castle built in Aragonese-Gothic style.

USEFUL ADDRESSES

HOTEL
Sardegna, tel. 869033

TOURIST INFORMATION
Piazza Marconi

La Maddalena

The island of La Maddalena, whose history has connections with two of the world's most famous warriors, Napoléon Bonaparte and Horatio Nelson, is a 15 minute boat trip from Palau, on Sardinia's north coast. With its archipelago, it was a vital defensive position in this part of the Mediterranean, and today houses the largest naval training establishment in Italy, plus a NATO base that can repair nuclear submarines.

La Maddalena's main shopping street, Via Azuni, is just behind the quayside, and through the alleyways there is a view of sparkling water and white ferry boats. The fishing harbour is round the corner from the ferry terminus at Cala Gavetta, as is the busy Piazza P. Tommaso which fronts on to it. Most of the hotels are beyond this point, a short walk from the town centre.

The town itself is a charming, prosperous place. There are two small harbours, with the ferry dock in between them. The one on the left is Cala Calvetta, where excursions to the other islands depart, and also buses for Caprera Island, which is linked to La Maddalena by a causeway, and to the rest of La Maddalena. Two blocks north of the port is the Piazza Garibaldi, from which runs the Via Garibaldi, the main shopping street.

EXCURSIONS
Beaches are everywhere, notably at Spalmatore and Cala Maiore on the northern side.

USEFUL ADDRESSES

TOURIST INFORMATION
24 Via XX Settembre, tel. 736321

HOTELS
Cala Lunga, at Porto Massimo, tel. 738096 (Pleasing resort hotel
  on the sea, with pool and beach)
Giuseppe Garibaldi, tel. 737314
Villa Marina, tel. 738340
Al Mare, tel. 738291
Excelsior, tel. 737020
Esit il Gabbiano, tel. 737007

RESTAURANTS
La Grotta, Via Principe di Napoli 3, tel. 737228 (One of the best
  on the island, specialising in seafood)
Mangana, tel. 738477
L'Araosta and Trattoria Marina (on the seafront)

TRAVEL AGENCIES
Conte e D'Oriano, Via Amendola 10, tel. 737660
Unimare, Via Garibaldi 56, tel. 738668

Lido Del Sole

Located on the scenic Gulf of Olbia, Lido del Sole is an
increasingly popular holiday resort, with expanding facilities for
the visitor. The view is dominated by the bulk of the Isola
Tavolara, one of a few uninhabited islands in the bay.

USEFUL ADDRESS

HOTEL
Caprile, tel. 42046

Luogosanto

Close to Luogosanto, down a country track, is the fascinating
location of Li Muri, a collective megalithic burial ground also

known as the 'giants' tomb.' It dates from the third millenium BC, to the period of the cult dedicated to the Mediterranean Mother Goddess, a cult that was common to all the peoples of the southern Mediterranean.

The tomb consists of a construction designed to house a number of corpses, and has a narrow corridor 13m long and 1m wide, with walls built of rock slabs that were originally covered with other slabs. The corpses were placed transversely in the tomb, in a crouching, almost fetal position. On the southern and narrower side of the construction is a large arc of vertical megalithic rock, between 1.5 and 2 metres in height.

Maracalagonis

A typical centre of the Cagliaria Campidano, the town of Maracalagonis has preserved all the characteristic features of ancient peasant architecture . . . arched doorways of dignified old houses opening onto the street, and houses built on the model of the Roman 'domus', with a large courtyard onto which open all the rooms, service areas, sheds for keeping agricultural implements and raw brick cellars for storing the delicate wines. The environment is enriched by a patio along the side of the houses, where the overhanging roof is surrounded by wooden pillars or columns.

Monte Sirai

On a plateau near the village of Sirai is Monte Sirai, where a Carthaginian settlement has recently been brought to light. This fortified settlement, the most imposing Carthaginian military discovery on the island, overlooks both the sea and the hinterland, showing that the founders were on guard against attack from both sea and land, and demonstrating how important the area was for Carthaginian strategy. The discoveries at Monte Sirai include not only fortifications but also traces of religious places and dwellings.

Muravera

An important centre of the Sarrabus area, with a largely
agricultural economy, Muravera is surrounded by vast citrus
groves in the coastal plain and along the mouth of the river
Flumendosa. Recently the area has been developed for tourism,
with hotels and apartments bordering the nearby beaches. Special
festivities celebrate the grape and citrus harvests.

USEFUL ADDRESSES

TOURIST INFORMATION
Piazza Europa 5, tel. 993760

HOTELS
Corallo, tel. 993502
Free Beach Club, tel. 991041, at Costa Rei, 3 km away
Colostrai, tel. 993658, at Torre Salinas, 8 km away

TRAVEL AGENCY
I.T.A., Corse Umberto, tel. 70828

Nora

The archaeological area of Nora is located on a promontory
overlooked by a 16th century tower built by Philip II that stood
guard against Saracen invaders and which is now a lighthouse.
From here visitors can admire the important remains of the town,
which was a commercial port founded by the Phoenicians with a
double harbour, one side sheltered from the west wind and the
others from the Mistral. First a Carthaginian and then a Roman
town, Nora declined and practically disappeared around the third
century AD apparently as a result of a disaster.
   Of the old town one can still see remains of the Carthaginian
warehouses, Roman buildings from the time of the Republic, a
Carthaginian-Roman temple, large baths with splendid mosaics
and a theatre that is almost intact, dating from the time of the

Empire. The system of water supply and drainage is particularly interesting, with large underwater pipes.

The sea around Nora still covers part of the town which sunk during an earthquake, but now piers and other buildings can be recognised due to the build up of marine deposits and the influence of the weather.

USEFUL ADDRESS

HOTEL
Su Guventeddu, tel. 9209092, at Pula

Nule

The name of this little village, whose economy is based on agriculture and sheep rearing, is known throughout Sardinia and even beyond it shores on account of the splendid carpets with strongly characterised designs produced by the local craftswomen. Tradition is reinforced by the activities of the Carpet-weavers' Co-operative ('Casa del Tappeto'), ISOLA Pilot Centre for crafts which, in addition to the production of carpets, provides training into the secrets of this ancient skill.

Nule carpets can be distinguished from other Sardinian pieces by their characteristic design and very bright colouring; the geometric designs are known as 'flames', and are reminiscent of Arab fabrics. Large carpets are woven here using a vertical loom, as opposed to the more conventional horizontal loom.

Up the hill is the old historic area with the church of Sant' Antioco, built in 1102 by the Benedictines of Saint-Victor at Marseilles, and whose catacombs, contrasting with the cavernous height of the church, are the resting place of the saint after whom the town is named. According to legend the most severe torture failed to kill him, and his frustrated executioners finally threw him into the sea to drown. That failed, too, and Antioco floated ashore at Sulcis where he converted the people and became their bishop.

Just outside the old town is a Punic-Roman necropolis and one of the most interesting small museums on the island, among whose Punic artefacts on display are a number of items decorated with mythical scenes, many toys of the children who perished, and pottery. There is also a tablet inscribed in Hebrew, testifying to the large number of Jewish settlers brought by the Romans, and some columns from the acropolis.

Not far from the town is the port of Calasetta, which boasts a charming and unusual sparkling white church that looks like a mosque, and straight streets making a geometrical square pattern. The main ones are wide enough for two cars to pass carefully, avoiding the water run-off in the centre, and all run down the hill to the port, round the corner of which is a little bay with a cluster of new villas. The harbour comes alive half a dozen times a day with the departure of the car ferry to the neighbouring island of San Pietro (a full day should be allowed for such an excursion).

Nuoro

The chief town of the province of the same name, Nuoro is situated at the heart of the most traditionally 'conservative' area of Sardinia with regard to dress and customs. It is, nevertheless, a modern town, constantly growing as a result of recent industrial development. Located on a plain at the foot of Monte Ortobene, Nuoro lies at the heart of an area that is one of the most important in Sardinia from the ethnological and naturalistic viewpoints. It has a tradition for culture, being the home town of one of Sardinia's heroines, the writer Grazia Deledda – who was awarded the Nobel Prize for Literature in 1926 and whose novels are evocations of Sardinian life – and the poet Sebastiano Satt, while the lively population has maintained a taste for friendly gatherings in bars, and for evening strolls.

One of the major attractions here is the Sardinian Folk Museum, where a series of architectural settings reproduce the building modules most typical of the various parts of the island. On display are costumes, jewellery, ornaments, work implements and furnishings characteristic of the people. The cultural life of the town includes various events, shows and conferences, with folk tradition reaching its peak at the end of August with the Feast of the Redeemer.

Perhaps more than any other Sardinian city, Nuoro is part of its province, without the sharp divisions between urbanities and country folk. Despite its magnificent mountain setting, it contains few historical sights as such, the interest in the city lying more in its people.

Nuoro's artistic life continues to flourish and has a real originality uninfluenced by invaders or conquerors. Almost everyone seems to lead a 'double-life', singing, writing or painting when there is any sort of pause in the work by which they earn a living. The few who put neither pen to paper nor brush to canvas are enthusiastic conversationalists, again reflecting their isolated region and independent lives, and the topics that dominate any talk are politics and banditry. They are completely honest about the latter, making no attempt to hide its existence, and indeed discuss the latest crime figures or well-known vendettas with a disarming frankness.

Indeed, banditry has been placed more in the category of quixotic outlawry than grand larceny, and until recently was a personal matter of Sard against Sard in the form of vengeance and vendetta, usually sparked off by cattle or sheep rustling. Now it is changing to people-stealing, rich industrialists and land-owners proving more lucrative in the way of ransom than animals. No alien stands a chance against the native mountain people, skilled as they are in living off the land – even if it is somebody else's land – and with an unparalleled knowledge of their hostile terrain. It was, and is, classic guerilla warfare, with a large number of carabinieri from the mainland having only limited success in combating crime figures.

The dogs which the Romans brought in to try to track down the Barbaracini, a corruption of the Roman term Barbaria, are still in the mountains, now converted to sheep dogs but looking no more friendly than centuries ago. Then, as now, livestock was all-important, but as there was very little fencing and few land-boundaries, the pigs, sheep and cows roamed freely making themselves easy targets for thieves.

At nearly 2,000 feet up, Nuoro is one of the highest cities in Italy, and the altitude makes for a cool, healthy climate. Even so, the Nuorese drive still higher to their playground on Monte Ortobene, a few miles through spectacular countryside and with the best hotels.

Two mountain villages, Orgosolo and Orune, share the dubious distinction of 'bandit capitals' of the island. From the former came a famous bandit who, like Robin Hood, was said to have robbed the rich to give to the poor.

PLACES OF INTEREST

Nearby
Splendid views can be enjoyed at Monte Ortobene, approximately
8 km away. The mountains also boasts a great bronze statue of the
Redeemer, dominating and protecting the mountain landscape.
   The district surrounding Nuoro contains much to interest the
visitor. To the north a remote, mountainous region, there is a
Nuraghic village with a sacred well near the town of Noddule; Bitti
is a large village, and Lula somewhat smaller, both with popular
festivals; while the valley of the River Posada, not traversed by any
road, and Monte Albo, to the south, are haunts of shepherds and
wild boar.

USEFUL ADDRESSES

FESTIVALS
A three-day summer festival is held at the end of July, called the
Sagra di San Pantaleo, and in August there is the Feast of the
Redeemer, another chance to see richly decorated costumes.

TOURIST INFORMATION
Piazza Italia 19, tel. 30083/32307

HOTELS
Grazia Deledda, Via Lamarmora 175, tel. 31257
Motel AGIP, Via Trieste, tel. 34071
Paradiseo, tel. 35585
Fratelli Sacchi, tel. 31200
Sandalia, Via Einaudi 14, tel. 38353

RESTAURANTS
Canne al Vento, Viale Repubblica 66, tel. 36641
Da Giovanni, Via Quattro Novembre 7, tel. 30562
Del Grillo, Via Monsignor Melas, tel. 32005
Fratelli Sacchi at Monte Ortobene, tel. 31200

CAR HIRE
Maggiore Autoservizi, Via Convento 32, tel. 30461
Staffa, Via Gramsci 4, tel. 33536

AUTOMOBILE CLUB
Via Sicilia 39, tel. 30034

TRAVEL AGENCIES
Ancor, Via Manzoni 85, tel. 30463
Barbagia Tours, Piazza Veneto 27, tel. 34579
Viaggi Avionave, Via Lamarmora 117, tel. 37446

OLBIA

Olbia, one of Sardinia's main points of entry, is situated by a deep bay, with fertile, level farmland behind it, and has reached a significant level of development with its port and airport; development that is partly due to the great number of tourist facilities in the north and south of the city and along the extremely beautiful coast.

Local cooking is largely influenced by the sea, though the products of the surrounding countryside are not disregarded, and there is an extensive range of attractive hotels, restaurants and other facilities for holiday makers.

USEFUL ADDRESSES

TOURIST INFORMATION
1 Via Castello Piro, tel. 21453

HOTELS
President, Via Principe Umberto 9, tel. 21551
De Plam, tel. 25777
Motel Olbia, tel. 51456
Royal, tel. 50253
Mediterraneo, tel. 24173
Li Cuncheddi, at Capo Ceraso, tel. 791163
Abi D'Oru, tel. 32001 and Sporting Hotel Palumbalza, tel. 34025, both at Marinella
Mare Bleu, tel. 39001 and Pozzo Sacro, tel. 21033, both at Pittulungu

RESTAURANTS
Tana del Drago, on road to Golfo degli Aranci, tel. 22777
Gallura, Corso Umberto, tel. 24648

TRAVEL AGENCIES
Agenzie Maritime Sarde, Via Acquedotto 52, tel. 24137
Avitur, Corso Umberto 139, tel. 21217
Intours, Corso Umberto 168, tel. 26069
Unimare, Via Principe Umberto 3, tel. 23572

Oliena

This large centre in the valley of the Cedrino, up against Monte
Corrasi which looms over it, is one of the best known towns in
Sardinia's interior, and the locally produced wine enjoys a high
reputation and is an excellent accompaniment to the traditional
roast dishes of the region.

Oliena's architecture is highly characteristic, with stone houses
such as are to be found in almost all the mountain villages. The
town takes its name from the nearby olive groves, while crafts,
popular tradition and folklore are still of the most authentic. A
famous element of the women's costumes is the heavy black
woollen shawl with silk fringes, completely hand-made and richly
embroidered with gold threads and semi-precious stones. Even
today it is not difficult to find houses where the people will open
their door to visitors and introduce them to the secrets of the
ancient art of hand-embroidery.

And there is no shortage of other houses willing to open their
doors . . . to allow you to sample the house produced wine.

Monte Corrasi is of great importance from the naturalistic point
of view, since it is the home of the last specimens of the
griffon-vulture. A great many moufflon also live there, and in late
autumn the sky is alive with the flights of millions of wood-pigeons
and doves.

Outside the town are two sanctuaries, those of Nostra Signora di
Monerrato, and San Giovanni. Near the latter is a natural spring
with a waterfall at Su Gologne, while above Oliena are the
Sopramonte, of which the tallest is Punta Corrasi, at 4,754 feet.

FESTIVAL
Good Friday sees a dramatic pageant, the Incontru (Encounter).

Oristano

The town of Oristano, which was recently promoted to the position of chief town of the province of the same name, is a lively commercial centre trading in the products of the fertile plain where farming and sheep-rearing flourish. Situated in a valley at the mouth of the river Tirso, it was the glorious capital of the medieval province of Arborea which held out relentlessly against the Aragonese invaders.

It is thought that Oristano was founded by the inhabitants of the Carthaginian-Roman town of Tharros, who were forced to abandon that site because of Saracen attacks about the year 1000. The town still has various features that recall its noble past, such as the Tower of San Cristoforo (also known as 'Mariano'), massive and powerful in its medieval construction; and an interesting example of 16th century civic building in the house known as 'Casa di Eleonora.' There are fine churches, too, especially that of Santa Chiara and the church of San Francesco, which contains a huge wooden cross known as the 'Crucifix of Nicodemus.' Then there is the Antiquarium Arborense, containing numerous archaeological exhibits from the neolithic period, the Nuraghic period, and Carthaginian and Roman times.

Oristano is a city of many qualities, and much subtlety. Its quiet and dignified air, and the orderliness and simplicity of its streets and buildings, make it seem almost otherworldly. Its walls were torn down long ago, and a circle of broad avenues surrounding the old town has replaced them: Via Mazzini, Via Solferini, Via Cagliari.

Oristano is also still very much the city of its most famous daughter, Sardinian heroine Eleonora d'Arborea, whose house can be seen at 4 Via Parpaglia and who is commemorated by a statue in the piazza named after her. It was the work of the Florentine sculptor Ulisse Cambi, and depicts Eleonora holding a copy of her famous Code of Laws and raising a declamatory hand. Lions sit at each corner and inset panels depict her victories both in war and peace.

Piazza Eleonora is linked by the pedestrians-only Corso Umberto I to Piazza Roma, the centre of Oristano, which with its trees and flowerbeds and through traffic is dominated by the Torre San Cristoforo, sometimes called Porta Manna or Torre di Mariano, after its builder. This tower of granite, with huge battlements and a smaller tower on top, and the Torre Portixdda, are all that remain of the fortified wall built in 1291.

Another link with Eleonora d'Arborea is the church of Santa Chiaro in Via Garibaldi where she is said to have been buried. The church was founded in the first half of the 14th century by the Giudice who handed over to Eleonora's father and has a simple exterior, while inside are five arches, a row of animal gargoyles projecting out from the walls, and a window behind the altar.

Much more imposing is the cathedral, which was begun in the early 13th century. It stands above the level of the Piazza del Duomo with a courtyard and trees, and you can see the base of the polygon bell-tower is one of the older sections. Most of the present church dates from 1733, with a Baroque interior, black and white tiled floor, and domes for every chapel. Next door to the cathedral is the Seminario Tridentino, founded in 1712, and the street is full of gracious old houses with elegant windows.

Very close by is the church of San Francesco, built in the 19th century by Gaetano Cima on the site of a Gothic church of which a couple of pillars remain.

Thanks to its position between the fertile plain and the nearby lagoons full of fish, Oristano, like all the neighbouring centres, offers a vast range of gastronomic delights, one of the local products being Vernaccia, a dry dessert wine with a high alcohol content.

Nearby
Nearby is the village of Santa Giusta, on the edge of the large pool of the same name, and clustered round an impressive basilica, one of the most illustrious monuments in Sardinia, dating from the 12th century. The pure lines of the simple façade in Lombard Romanesque style are in complete harmony with the arches, corbels and pilaster strips on the sides of the temple, the apse and the mighty bell-tower. The austere interior is perhaps even more interesting, with three naves supported by columns in different styles, from the nearby Carthaginian–Roman centres, while the large crypt is also supported by columns that once belonged to Roman buildings.

FESTIVALS
Probably the most spectacular of the pre-Lenten carnivals held in Sardinia is the 'Sa Sartiglia,' in Oristano, which is a costumed parade and tournament introduced by the Spaniards but since given a strange Sardinian flavour. Among the displays of equestrian prowess, a rider wearing a costume with red ribbons tied on his arms and legs, a feminine mask and a top hat, gallops at full speed towards a silver star suspended from a ribbon, and tries to impale it with a short spear!

Other festivals in the town include the Sagra di Santa Croce, from September 11–14, which combines religious celebrations with a lively fair.

USEFUL ADDRESSES

TOURIST INFORMATION
Via Cagliari 276, tel. 74191

HOTELS
Mistral, tel. 212505
Amiscora, tel. 72503
Ca-Ma, tel. 74374
I.S.A., tel. 78040
Piccolo, tel. 71500
Del Sole, at Torre Grande, tel. 22000

RESTAURANTS
Il Faro, Via Bellini 25, tel. 70002
La Forchetta d'Oro, Via Giovanni Ventitresimo, tel. 70462
Da Giovanni, at Torre Grande beach, Via Colombo 8, tel. 22051
Stella Marina, Via Tirso 6, tel. 72506

TRAVEL AGENCIES
Sardatur, Via Mazzini 8 tel. 74307
Tharros, Via Cagliari 268, tel. 73389

CAR HIRE
Contini, Via Masones 18, tel. 73489
Fara Viaggi, Via Othoca 72, tel. 72883
Lombardi, Via Carmine 7, tel. 78289

Orosei

The village of Orosei, which the Romans called Fanum Carisii, lies at the mouth of the Cedrino with a fertile stretch between sea and mountains. There is an impressive old tower, part of the medieval castle, and from the Piazza del Popolo a steep flight of steps leads to the Primiziale church, which seems to have expanded into three quite separate sections.

Ozieri

An attractive small town built in a circle in a sheltered valley, with stone buildings and colonnades, Ozieri conserves a touch of nobility in its architecture, as well as being one of Sardinia's most important centres for cheese production and sheep, cattle and horse breeding. Nearby at Chilivani there are stables for horse breeding and a racecourse where meetings are held.

There is a fine tradition of cooking here, based on local farm products. Try if you can to sample the famous 'suspiros' cakes, made of ground almonds wrapped in coloured paper. Ozieri also has an intense cultural life, and the most prestigious literary prize for Sardinian prose and poetry is given here.

The cathedral, built in the 16th century but rebuilt three centuries later, contains works by a 16th century painter known as the 'Master of Ozieri' along with some by the 'Master of Castelsardo'; it also contains a painting of the Last Supper by Giovanni Marghinotti who lived in the first half of the 19th century, and a 16th century silver Gothic cross. In the town are many fine small palaces with loggias, and a beautiful fountain in the Piazza Grisoni.

Of particular interest to the visitor is the new archaeology museum containing Nuraghic discoveries from the many sites in the region as well as Punic and Roman items.

Near Ozieri, at Burghidu, is a Nuraghic castle containing a sacred well and the remains of a tower.

FESTIVAL
Madonna del Remedio on 29 September

USEFUL ADDRESSES

HOTEL
Mastino, tel. 787041

TRAVEL AGENCY
Intours, Piazza Garibaldi, tel. 787142

Palau

The point of embarkation for the island of La Maddalena, Palau is
well equipped with bars, boutiques, shops, craftsmen's 'ateliers'
and restaurants, and is popular with tourists staying in hotels and
villas along the bay, especially in the evenings and on market day.
The charm of the marine views, the cordiality of the people and the
reminders of Garibaldi at Caprera make a detour to the
archipelago of La Maddalena well worthwhile. In the summer,
boats depart from La Maddalena several times daily; tickets can be
obtained from Tirrenia, Piazza del Molo, tel. 709270, or aboard
the various boats.

USEFUL ADDRESSES

TOURIST INFORMATION
92 Via Nazionale, tel. 709570

HOTELS
Del Molo, tel. 708042
Excelsior Vanna, tel. 709589
La Roccia, tel. 709528
Piccada, tel. 709344
Serra, tel. 709519

Paulilatino

Interesting domestic architecture characterises this small town, beside the doors of whose houses one can still see the stone mounting blocks and the rings, sometimes made of stone, for tethering horses and pack animals. Paulilatino also boasts an interesting folk museum containing a display of tools and domestic implements once used in the area, and visitors can buy interesting local crafts at the ISOLA pilot centre for crafts.

The area around the town is particularly rich in tombs, and contains the famous Holy Well of Santa Christina, widely considered one of the most fascinating and mysterious traces of early Sardinian civilisation. The well is admirably made, with a staircase by which the celebrants could reach the water level. Even today the construction is considered astonishing for its perfection of form and volume. Around it are the exedra and the sacred enclosure, and nearby the remains of civic buildings, the dwellings of the novices, and market place. About 100 metres from the wall area there is a nuraghe and some interesting tombs, which are sign-posted.

The country church of Santa Christina, the nearby cottages for the novices, and a refreshment area echo today the layout of the old sanctuary.

Nearby is the Nuraghe Losa, one of the biggest and best preserved in Sardinia. The gigantic fortress stands around the old central tower and is made up of a labyrinth of walls, wall walks, spiral staircases, alcoves and open-air restaurants.

Porto Rafael

At the heart of the magnificent bay of Palau lies the tiny village of Porto Rafael where an arcaded piazza opens onto one of many sandy coves fringed with smooth, silver rocks. Around it, bougainvillea and geraniums cling to white-washed villas with pinnacled roofs, and wherever you turn the view is enchanting.

Porto Rafael has a charm and individuality unlike anywhere else in Sardinia. The village has retained its distinctive and somewhat exclusive character, with life revolving lazily around the piazza . . .

a gossip at the well-stocked supermarket, an aperitif at Harry's Bar, a game of tennis at the tiny yacht club. In July and August an excellent, if expensive, restaurant opens up to complement slightly less extensive establishments, as well as a little discothèque in the piazza.

Palau, the nearest town, offers a good range of shops and restaurants with a weekly market, while a regular ferry service operates to La Maddalena, the largest of the beautiful offshore islands in the bay, which also has an attractive and well-stocked shopping centre.

Porto Rotondo

This fashionable little resort was conceived by a group of friends who created the original centre around a natural harbour about 20 years ago. It lies about 12 miles south of the Costa Smeralda, which it faces across the water, on a lovely stretch of coastline dotted with sandy beaches, and has become a lively little resort, very much oriented to the sea and boats. Its busy marina makes a charming focal point, and there is a choice of smart restaurants and bars as well as fashionable boutiques.

USEFUL ADDRESSES

HOTELS
Relais Sporting, tel. 34005 (One of the smartest in the area, and a favourite with discerning holidaymakers; it is a 28-room hotel, splendidly set on a small promontory enclosing the marina).
San Marco, tel. 34108
Aldia Manna, tel. 34049

TRAVEL AGENCY
Porto Rotondo Viaggi, Via Molo

Portoscuso

Portoscuso, a port with an Aragonese tower and a beach, unites the various components of the old civilizations of this area, divided between an industrial mining world, peasant tradition and marine activities. In this area there are important mining installations, processing industries, fertile vineyards and installations on land and sea for tunny fishing. The latter activity, which had been abandoned for the past decade, has now been revived and is a valuable source of income.

From Portoscuso there are car-ferries to the very pretty village of Carloforte on the island of San Pietro, while also of interest is the Nuraghic village of Serrucci, where some of the buildings are virtually intact.

USEFUL ADDRESSES

TOURIST INFORMATION
Piazza del Vecchio Municipio, tel. 509504

HOTELS
Panorama, tel. 508077
Costa del Sole, tel. 508123
Mistral, tel. 509230
S'Alegusto, tel. 509017

TRAVEL AGENCY
Portur, Via Giulio Cesare 77, tel. 509234

Porto Torres

Porto Torres, one of the prime tourism ports in Sardinia, dates back to the Carthaginian era and was a Roman colony, as the many impressive remains from this period indicate. With its ferry services to Genoa, Livorno and Civitavecchia, Porto Torres is a bustling place, and one with a considerable amount of interest for the visitor. There is a fine Roman bridge over the River Turritano whose seven arches decrease in size to accommodate the different height of either bank, and there is an unkempt Roman ruin containing baths, columns, bits of mosaics, etc, and the remains of the 'Barbarians' Palace' whose origins are uncertain but which is thought to have begun life as a temple to the Goddess of Fortune.

There are beaches near the town at Marinella and Platamona, a lido popular with the Sassarese, and on the road to Sassari many nuraghi and a Neolithic sanctuary at Monte Accodi, with tombs, remains of temples, two menhirs, and a great altar.

FESTIVAL
Procession of San Gavino, held during the first week of June, when the residents walk from the basilica to the chapel of San Gavino a Mare, perched on a clifftop.

USEFUL ADDRESSES

TOURIST INFORMATION
Piazza Colombo

HOTELS
La Casa, tel. 514288
Libissonis, tel. 501613
Torres, tel. 510604

RESTAURANT
Ristorante Cristallo, Via XX Settembre

CAR HIRE
Barraghini, Via Petronia 4, tel. 514928
Lentinu, Via Balai 15, tel. 514276
Maggiore, Via Losto, tel. 514652

Quartu S. Elena

Quartu S. Elena is now basically a suburb of Cagliari, but it rather endearingly refuses to accept the fact, and instead valiantly struggles to maintain its individuality and separateness. Of interest to the sightseer is a 13th century Romanesque church built in the cemetery of another.

USEFUL ADDRESSES

HOTELS
Diran, tel. 815271
Califfo, tel. 890131, at Foxi
Setar, tel. 890001, at S'Oru e Mari
Costa degli Angeli-Park Hotel, tel. 807253, at Santa Luria

Samassi

A large centre in the Campidano, with a well-developed agricultural economy, Samassi preserves a great many characteristics that were once found in all the villages in the area. One example is the use today in domestic architecture of bricks made from mud and straw and dried in the sun; these are highly resistant to the elements yet cost almost nothing to make.

USEFUL ADDRESSES

TOURIST INFORMATION
36 Viale Caprera, tel. 233729

Sanluri

A pleasant little agricultural town, Sanluri is of interest for its typical domestic architecture, while especially noteworthy is the castle, pointing to the medieval origins of the town, and of which a square formation with battlemented towers is still fairly well preserved and restored. Located in the centre of the town, the castle was built around the 14th century by the Malaspina family and played an important part in the valiant defence of the medieval province of Arborea against Aragon. One of Sardinia's most habitable castle, despite its stern square battlements, it is today the home of an interesting museum, organised by the owner, and containing relics of the First World War and the colonial wars.

Restaurants in Sanluri offer plenty of opportunities for trying out the local specialities, particularly the 'bread of Sanluri', which comes in big, swollen loaves.

USEFUL ADDRESSES

TOURIST INFORMATION
Via Carlo-Felice

HOTELS
Mirage, tel. 9307100
Motel Ichnusa, tel. 9307073

TRAVEL AGENCY
Neltourist, 9 Via Umberto 1, tel. 9307026

AUTOMOBILE CLUB
Piazza Vittoria Emanuele 13, tel. 9307171

San Pietro

The island of San Pietro is smaller than its neighbour, Sant'Antioco – a mere six miles long and five miles wide. Its harbour of Carloforte, an extremely pretty town of pastel-coloured houses, has two boat services, one to the mainland where the crossing to Portovesme takes 40 minutes and operates frequently from dawn until late evening in summer, and the other from the neighbouring isle. The saint after whom the island is named is supposed to have been shipwrecked here on his way to Cagliari and to have taught the inhabitants how to catch fish with harpoons and nets.

Life in Carloforte centres on the Via Toma, the shady esplanade containing most of the restaurants, and the town is becoming very popular with tourists.

Today, vegetable couscous, an inheritance from Tabarca, is the regular Sunday lunch of the visitors who come over from the mainland, paying little more than the price of a couple of cups of coffee for their fare, to join the islanders on their traditional promenade. Lobsters, sardines and prawns also make up the menus in the waterfront restaurants, with the addition of a special fish soup flavoured with basil, nuts and garlic.

From Carloforte a winding road crosses the centre of the island, past Guardia dei Mori, the highest point, where the Saracens are said to have had a fortress, through pine woods to Cala Filo. There are beaches along the western coast, where another road connects the town with La Caletta. Two grottoes on the coast, at Mezzaluna and Punta delle Oche, can be reached only by sea; excursions are arranged from the harbour at Carloforte.

At the southern tip of the island is the San Vittoria tower, housing an important astronomical observatory.

USEFUL ADDRESSES

HOTELS
Hieracon, tel. 854028
Riviera, tel. 854004
Paola, tel. 854898

RESTAURANT
Tre Archi di Augusto, Via Colombo, Carloforte

Sant'Antioco

The 'island' of Sant'Antioco, rich in history, is one of the oldest centres in Sardinia. Founded by the Phoenicians, it then became an important Carthaginian and Roman town for the control of the sea to the south of Sardinia. Today, linked to the mainland by a causeway, it is a popular seaside resort, containing traces of the ancient civilisations that dominated this area.

The most important discovery is the Phoenician-Carthaginian funerary area ('Tophet') where the urns containing the remains of the first-born sacrificed to the god Bes are still scattered around.

172

Beside the necropolis are the excellently preserved remains of a Carthaginian temple, while the area is dominated by a Carthaginian-Roman fort.

The economy of Sant'Antioco is based on activities connected with the nearby mining area, on the production of excellent wines, and on tourists who are attracted by the beautiful coastline, interesting beaches, rocks, marine caves and vegetation. The sea surrounding it is rich in fish, promising anglers a good catch.

USEFUL ADDRESSES

TOURIST INFORMATION
Piazza de Gasperi

HOTELS
I Ciclopi, tel. 80087, at Sapone
La Fazenda, tel. 83477, at Capo Sperone
Maladroxia, tel. 82611, at Maladroxia

RESTAURANTS
Da Nicola, Lungomare Vespucci, tel. 83286
La Torre, Via Marconi 1 at Calasetta, tel. 88466

SANTA MARGHERITA DI PULA

The holiday resort of Santa Magherita di Pula is one of the most important in Sardinia, and is a particular favourite with British holidaymakers, not least since it houses the enormous Forte holiday village, first opened in 1971 and since developed considerably.

Set on the sun-drenched south coast, behind a stretch of soft, warm sand enclosed by 55 acres of pines, the complex boasts extravagant gardens and miles of plant-bordered paths. The choice and variety of activities and pursuits for the holidaymaker is huge; there are bars to suit every taste and time of day; music and dancing go on until late at the Rocca Bar and discothèque; the Oasis and Scorpion bars add to the enjoyment of the sea and pools – and the pools add enjoyment to breakfast, as does the music.

After dinner the Piazza Maria Luigia comes alive as the sun goes down. Here one can sip a long cool drink, or look around the bazaars and boutiques, where there is everything for sale from toothpaste to clothes. Later in the evening one can watch an open-air show, professionally staged with musicians, dancers and special artistes.

The Forte village has three restaurants that overlook the pools, or the sea, or the mountains, and for those catering for their own meals there are five bars and snack bars. Between the beach and the square is a supervised play centre where children have their own pool, adventure playground, games and a couple of clubs open from morning until evening. Other amenities include cartoons and a children's shop, as well as trampolining; there is an all-day nursery for babies, and baby-sitters are also available.

Teenagers, too, have their own club and club house, with activities throughout the day geared to suit their age group; while for the sportive, facilities include the beach, tennis (12 hard courts

174

floodlit at night and four half-courts), bowling, croquet, ping pong, soccer, open-air squash, swimming, trampolines, volleyball, basketball, waterpolo and sauna. Coaches are available for instruction and advice in most major sports. Watersports include sailing boats, windsurfers, scuba diving, parasailing, water-skiing and boat excursions, and car hire is available from the village reception.

The complex also includes the elegant Hotel Castello, whose bedrooms are air-conditioned, spacious and tastefully decorated in Mediterranean style, and equipped with telephone, private bathroom with bath and shower attachment, WC, bidet and handbasin. Room service is available for breakfast, snacks and drinks, and the hotel has its own restaurant and piano bar.

USEFUL ADDRESSES

HOTELS
Forte Village, tel. 921531
Castello Hotel, tel. 921531

OTHER HOTELS
Abamar, tel. 921555
Flamingo, tel. 9208361
Is Morus, tel. 921434
Mare e Pinta, tel. 9209407

Santa Teresa Di Gallura

It is from the port and holiday resort of Santa Teresa di Gallura that holidaymakers choosing Sardinia as a base can take a ferry boat across to the island of Corsica; the journey takes about an hour, and services operate several times a day in the peak summer period. Tickets and details of sailing times can be obtained from: Tirrenia, Via Porto 51, tel. 754156

Superb sandy beaches surround this pleasant little town, perched on a panoramic headland at the north eastern tip of Sardinia. The coastline is really spectacular here with a narrow finger of land bordered by beautiful beaches leading to the promontory of Capo

Testa, where incredible rock formations of silver and white granite rise from the brilliantly clear water.

One fortification only is left in Santa Teresa today: the 16th century Torre Longosardo built by the Spanish King Philip II and overlooking the fine beach of Rena Bianca, the resort area where holidaymakers have one of the finest views of Corsica to the north-east, and which is guarded by a Spanish watchtower.

The little town sits on top of the hill and does not overlook the beach. In the Piazza San Vittoria is a 19th century church, while the hub is the Piazza Vittorio Emanuele I, its centre paved and tree-lined. The third section of Santa Teresa is the port, which retains the old name of Porto Longone, and is situated a mile away with a long creek where boats tie up.

The most interesting aspect of the port is that the development is on one side only: the quayside, with its tamarisk trees, lobsters awaiting export and bustle of arriving ferries. Across the water is simply hill countryside, giving the impression that the smaller boats have found the sheltered natural anchorage by accident and moored where they please.

Santa Teresa is well equipped in its own right, with a good shopping centre and a choice of restaurants; however, public transport is non-existent, so a car is recommended for choosing this resort as a base for exploration.

FESTIVALS
Sant'Antonio, in early June; and Santa Teresa from 14–16 October.

USEFUL ADDRESSES

TOURIST INFORMATION
Piazza Vittorio Emanuele, tel. 754127

HOTELS
Moresco, tel. 754188
Bacchus, tel. 754556
Belvedere, tel. 754160
Corallaro, tel. 754341
Esit Miramare, tel. 754103
Li Nibbari, tel. 754453
Capo Testa e Dei du Mari, tel. 754333, at Capo Testa
Hotel Villagio Santa Teresa, tel. 751520, at Marmorata

RESTAURANTS
Canne al Vento, Via Nazionale 23, tel. 754219
Mistral, on Capo Testa road, tel. 754490
Riva, Via del Porto, tel. 754392

TRAVEL AGENCIES
Agenzie Maritime Sard, Piazza del Porto, tel. 754156
Sandorma, Via Lamarmora, tel. 754464
Sardinia Tours, Via XX Settembre 14, tel. 754657
Sangri La, Via Nazionale

AUTOMOBILE CLUB
Zona del Porto, tel. 754196

San Teodoro

San Teodoro has become a popular holiday resort in recent years, not only because of its attractive setting and pleasant beach but because, like nearby Budoni, it is considerably less expensive than the Costa Smeralda which lies to the north.

USEFUL ADDRESSES

TOURIST INFORMATION
Via Sardegna

HOTELS
Due Lune, tel. 864075
Bungalow Hotel, tel. 865786
Scintilla, tel. 865519
Mimose, tel. 865763
Onda Marina, tel. 865788
Sandalion, tel. 865753
San Teodoro, tel. 865680

Santu Antine

Santu Antine contains the imposing building known as the 'Nuraghe Palace', one of the most significant examples of prehistoric remains in Sardinia, testifying to the level of civilisation and technology achieved by the Nuraghic people. Around the original tower three other defence towers were added, all with loopholes which were blocked in at a later period by the addition of a surrounding wall which formed a fortified curtain round the towers. The oldest tower is three storeys tall, the last of these being open, and at the base are passageways leading to wider walks along the fortified curtain. It is possible to visit the wall-walks and the upper part of the nuraghe by means of external staircases, as well as by the spiral staircases inside.

This well preserved monument has an internal fortified courtyard and a deep well. Around the fortress are the remains of Carthaginian and Roman buildings, indicating the fact that the structure was used over a long period of time.

The Santu Antine nuraghe, along with other fortresses in the area, was designed to form part of an integrated system of defence.

Sardara

A large village located between the Campidano plain and the hills of Marmilla, Sardara is well known for the thermal springs of Santa Maria des Aquas, 3 km away. Here there are five hot springs of sodium bicarbonate water, in a charming setting amid pine and eucalyptus woods. Interesting sights in Sardara include the nuraghe temple and well of Sant'Anastasia next to the little church of the same name, and the 13th century church of San Gregorio. Craft products are well developed, particularly carpets, which are excellently woven to an original design.

Nearby is the town of San Gavino Monreale which, alongside its modern civic buildings, has maintained much of the old domestic architecture typical of the area. Saffron is still grown in these parts, though on a much smaller scale than it used to be.

Between Sardara and San Gavino, on a hill 260 metres high, stand the remains of the Castle of Monreale, one of the fortresses of the Giudice of Arborea, controlling by its position all communications between Oristano and Cagliari.

USEFUL ADDRESSES

HOTEL
Delle Terme, tel. 934025

SASSARI

Sassari is one of the most appealing towns to be found in Sardinia. Its origins are uncertain, although documents concerning the existence of the city go back to the 12th century AD. What does seems likely is that the area was well populated in prehistoric times, judging from the numerous remains found in the countryside surrounding the city. Sassari had a great political role during its history as a defender of freedom: it survived for a long period as a 'free city' though allied with Pisa and later with Genoa, and was the centre of the so-called 'Angione revolt', the attempt to import the ideals of the French Revolution into Sardinia.

Sassari is Sardinia's second city in regard to population and importance, and is differentiated from other towns of the island in terms of architecture, urban planning and physiognomy, recalling a city in Tuscany or central Italy. For example, it is the only city in Sardinia that has a real 'piazza' – not only the geographical centre but also the cultural, social and political heart of the city.

Sassari somehow manages to be very Sardinian in character, yet different from anywhere else on the island. There is still very much the air of a medieval free city here: the civic spirit is reflected, for example, in the 'Festival of the Candlesticks', organised each year by the ancient guilds, as well as in the buildings themselves, and in the jewel of the medieval town that is the historic centre.

Three almost contiguous squares connect the old town with the new. Piazza Italia is a 19th century creation, with the obligatory statue of Vittorio Emanuele, and a stately sandstone building housing the offices of the provincial government. Across the square is the Giardino Palace which, though not a palace, and of relatively recent construction, is a splendid work in a type of Victorian Gothic style. A bank and the tourist information office share the ornate interior.

Next comes the Piazza Cavallino de Honestis, often referred to by its old name, Piazza Castello, which now holds Sassari's skyscraper buildings and many cafés, but which once held an Aragonese castle, and which marks the boundary between modern Sassari and the original walled city, full of medieval streets.

North of Corso Vittorio Emanuele, the main thoroughfare of the old town, is another fine square, Piazza Tola, named after two brothers, Sardinian patriots of the 19th century with, at its southern end, the 16th century Palazzetto Usini and the Music Conservatory.

Sassari now is quite a sophisticated place, but it has not lost touch with the countryside. Two bridges off the Corso Trinita carry the city over to its northern extension, but beneath them, in a narrow valley, farmers still plant their crops. Down here, accessible by steps from the Rosello bridge, is the Rosello Fountain, symbol of Sassari which looks more like a stage-set than a fountain, decorated with figures representing the four seasons, dolphins and gargoyles.

South of the Corso in a maze of winding streets is the cathedral of San Nicola, originally a 13th century structure, of which only the campanile remains. The church was completely rebuilt in the 15th century while, in the 1700s, the famous Baroque façade was added. The church has been restored to its 15th century style, though its best external feature is a magnificent Baroque façade. The interior, with a modern rose window above the altar, contains much of interest, especially the marble font from Piedmont with clawed feet and, in contrast, a simple wooden madonna above the altar.

Around the corner, on Via Santa Caterina, is another fine building, the 18th century Ducal Palace, originally owned by the Duke of Asinara, and heavily restored in 1775. The reception rooms are an informal museum with works of art and a valuable collection of Sard costume dolls by Eugenio Tavolara.

In the city's pleasant Giardino Pubblico is a modern handicrafts pavilion, with exhibits of Sard handicrafts, most of which are on sale. The island's raw materials, such as dwarf palm, clay, cork, wood, silver are transformed into baskets, jars, bridal chests, carpets, filigree jewellery, food, drink and wine.

Alongside the gardens is the University, which was maintained by the Jesuits after it had been founded in 1588 by Alessio Fontana, secretary to Carlo V. Today's faculties of medicine and veterinary science are famous, and the library contains more than 100,000 volumes, including Latin and Spanish manuscripts.

On Via Roma, main street of the modern part of town, is the Museo Archaeologico Sanno, displaying art and artefacts of all the periods of early Sardinian history. Especially interesting are the exhibits on the shadowy Neolithic people who preceded the Nuraghic builders, with finds from their important religious site at Anghela Ruiu near Sassari. In a separate part of the museum is a wonderful exhibition of Sardinian costumes, crafts and folk art.

The traditions of cooking in Sassari are intense, and ancient popular recipes are still used.

FESTIVALS
The city is well known for its folk festivities, especially the Sardinian Cavalcade and the feast of 'Li Candelieri', and is the capital of Sardinian craftsmanship, with a bi-annual exhibition of arts and crafts held here as well as a permanent exhibition showing the finest examples of artistic and practical craft from all over the island.

The Cavalcade, held on Ascension Day, has become one of the most popular festivals on the island; a showcase for costumes, songs and poetry of all Sardinian villages.

Li Candelieri, on 14 August, is something different: it is not of religious origin at all, but a ritual of a medieval civitas unusual in southern Europe. The main event is the procession of the medieval guilds, each group carrying a candlestick decorated with emblems of the guild and its patron saint, and includes an act of submission of the city officials to the leader of the farmers' guild, on whom the life of this city has depended.

Nearby
The beautiful Romanesque-Pisan church of the Santissima Trinita di Saccargia, built in the 12th century; a castle built by the noble Malaspina family at Osilo, in the mountains just east of Sassari; and a petrified forest near Martis.

EXCURSIONS
Sassari's station, at Piazza Stazione on the western edge of the old town, is the centre for rail connections in the province. FS trains for Porto Torres, Olbia, Oristano and the south leave from here, as well as the Strade Ferrate Sarde narrow-gauge trains for the Alghero-Tempio Pausanio-Palau route. This line, whose trains are more like trams, passes through some wonderful scenery, and provides a delightful excursion through the Gallura region.

Buses depart from the Emiciclo Garibaldi Piazza.

USEFUL ADDRESSES

TOURIST INFORMATION
Via Brigita Sassari, tel. 233534
Viale Caprera 36, tel. 233729/233751

HOTELS
Grazia Deledda, Viale Dante 47, tel. 271235
Frank, Via Diaz 20, tel. 276456
Marine Due, Via Chironi, tel. 277282

RESTAURANTS
Gallo d'Oro, Piazza d'Italia 3, tel. 230044
Il Senato, Via Mundula 2, tel. 231423
Tre Stelle, Via Porcellana 6, tel. 232431
La Forchette Sarda, Via Cagliari
Ziromira, Largo Sisini

CAR HIRE
Acanfora, Viale Caprera 8/a, tel. 291113
Autobus Grindi Bus, Grattacielo, tel. 234742
Autonoleggio Italia, Viale M. Coppino 2, tel. 238079
Ciccotti, Via Alghero 22, tel. 274019; Via Tempio 8, tel. 276334
Demontis Autonoleggi, via Mazzini 2, tel. 235547
Grindi Bus Organizz. Viaggi e C., Via B. Croce 1, tel. 219494;
     Emiciclo Garibaldi, tel. 234742
Hertz, Via Spano 1/3, tel. 236261; Via Michele Coppino 2,
     tel. 235244
Maggiore Autoservizi, Viale Italia 3, tel. 235507
Nolauto Sarda, Via IV Novembre, tel. 276788
Poddighe, Via G. Spano 1, tel. 236261
Sardinia, Viale Dante 29/a, tel. 274367

TRAVEL AGENCIES
Agitour, Piazza Italia 7, tel. 236952
Ajo Viaggi, Via E. Costa 60
Lorviaggi, Viale Dante 29/a, tel. 271489
Olvia, Viale Italia 7/c, tel. 238007
Sardaviaggi, Via Cagliari 44, tel. 234498
Voligam, Via Muroni 14; tel. 238203

AUTOMOBILE CLUB
Viale Adua 32, tel. 270070

AIR TERMINAL
Via Cagliari 30

Siniscola

An old agricultural town famous for its women's costumes,
Siniscola is becoming the centre of a major new holiday area, with
a wide, sandy beach at La Caletta, and another by the old fishing
village of Santa Lucia. Further to the north is a headland, Capo
Comino, with the nuraghe Artora, and further south another
resort, Cala Liberotto, with yet another nuraghe in the hills above
it.

USEFUL ADDRESSES

HOTELS
Montalbo, tel. 878548
L'Aragosta, tel. 810129; La Caletta, tel. 810077 and Villa Pozzi at
    La Caletta
Tirrno, tel. 91007; Cala Ginepro, tel. 91047, and Sa Mattanosa,
    tel. 91070, at Cala Liberotto.

Sinis

Sinis is a low, flat peninsula northwest of Oristano, covered mainly
in heather, and well worth going out of your way to visit although,
as there are no buses to Sinis, you will need your own transport.
Separated from the rest of the island by the Stagno di Cabras, a
lagoon full of fish and eels, Sinis is an attractive place, with a
wealth of interesting things to see.

Not far from the town, for example, is the Sanctuary of San
Salvatore, surrounded by a 'festival village' which, deserted for
most of the year, springs to life in September for the annual
festival. The church is built on an ancient religious site; a trapdoor
in the floor leads to a 4th century sanctuary dedicated to Hercules

Soter, with Roman frescoes portraying Venus and Cupid, and Hercules slaying a serpent.

At the southern tip of the peninsula is the fishing village of San Giovanni in Sinis, a place which the 20th century seems to have passed by. The village consists of a long row of huts along the shore, built according to an age-old highly aesthetic design and made of rushes which the fishermen also use to build their boats. The parish church of San Giovanni is, after San Saturnino in Cagliari, the oldest in Sardinia, dating from the 5th century; and like San Saturnino and all the early Christian monuments in Sardinia it is in the form of a Greek cross with a dome over the centre. Of particular interest is an original baptismal font, carved with a fish at the bottom.

Close to the village are the excavations of Tharros, part of which, as at Nora, is underwater. On the hill overlooking the town are the Punic necropolis and tophet, a Spanish tower of the 15th century and the remains of a synagogue, and there are several pleasant beaches in the vicinity.

On the western coast of Sinis is another large beach of multicoloured pebbles, with a view of the uninhibited island mysteriously known as Mal di Ventre (stomachache) and peculiar rock formations further up the coast.

Sinnai

This large centre still maintains its character as a rich farming village of the Cagliari hinterland. Although modern buildings have spread into the outskirts, many houses in the old part of the town retain their original appearance, and even some of the newer ones are a combination of Carthaginian and Roman architectural styles, using traditional building methods. Traditions are religiously observed here, and most families keep and treasure their fine old costumes, excellently made with an abundance of brocades, velvets, lace embroidery and jewels, even though they are now worn only on very special occasions.

The 'capital' of almond production, Sinnai produces a delicious range of cakes, the chief ingredient of which is ground almonds flavoured with orange blossom. Among the typical craft products are baskets for many uses, especially little straw cases decorated with brocades and bows. A fine pinewood stands close to the village.

USEFUL ADDRESSES

TOURIST INFORMATION
Via Funtanalada

STINTINO

One of Sardinia's fastest-growing holiday resorts is Stintino, located on a narrow peninsula dotted with lagoons at the northwestern corner of Sardinia. It is a fishing village that has developed considerably over the past few years, and is still developing apace, thanks to its lovely setting, and it now boasts a good selection of hotels, restaurants and shops.

Settled at the end of the 19th century by fishermen and shepherds from the nearby island of Asinara, which became a penal colony, Stintino has a double cove to take its fishing fleet and an increasing number of smart yachts and motor boats. As well as tunny-fishing, there are lobster pots specially designed to return unharmed to the sea the small and young specimens.

Beyond the village begins an extensive development of scattered and luxurious villas whose owners have one of the most beautiful beaches on the island, that of La Pelosa, with white sand and turquoise water. At land's end is Capo Falcone, where underwater fishing contests take place, and on top of the hill, covered with scrub to soften the rocks, is the Torre Falcone, erected by the Spanish.

Sitting squatly between the cape and the tiny Isola Piana is the island of Asinara, only ten miles long and four miles wide; the Romans called it Sinuaria, and it looks like four separate islands rather than one. Its name is derived from its wild asses which in their turn produced a breed of albino donkeys which survive today.

EXCURSIONS
From Stintino interesting excursions can be made to Porto Torres and its nearby prehistoric site of Monte d'Accoddi; and the 'Nuraghic Palace' at Santu Antine, one of the most striking and best preserved nuraghe in Sardinia.

USEFUL ADDRESSES

HOTELS
Ancora Residence, tel. 527085
Cala Reale, tel. 523127
Cala Regina, tel. 523126
Hotel Sporting, tel. 527187
Rocca Ruja, at Capo Falcone, tel. 527038
Geranio Rosso, tel. 523292
La Pelosetto, tel. 527188

RESTAURANTS
Marina Piccola, Via Cala d'Oliva
Capo Falcone, at La Pelosa, tel. 527039 (offering a superb view)

TRAVEL AGENCY
Stintours, Via Cala Reale, tel. 523160

Tempio Pausania

The cordiality and good humour of the inhabitants of Tempio Pausania, located at an altitude of 1,500 feet, make this a pleasant town for the holidaymaker to visit, and its rivers are particularly popular with trout fishermen.

The town's focal point is Piazza Gallura, a handsome square with the town hall taking up the whole of one side, while in Piazza San Pietro there is a 15th century Aragonese-Romanesque cathedral of the same name, restored in the 19th century but retaining the original carved wooden door and steeple. Also in the piazza is the Oratory, with an elegant Romanesque facade and a roof that curves up to enfold the bell in the middle.

Tempio Pausania is also noted for the severe dress of its female residents, its sparkling wine, and its local culinary specialities, particularly sausages.

FESTIVAL
In February a festival is held here known as Corsi Mascherati, which celebrates the death of King Carnival. There are bonfires and floats, and white wine is offered to the public.

USEFUL ADDRESSES

TOURIST INFORMATION
Piazza Gallura 2

HOTELS
Delle Sorgenti, tel. 630033
Petit Hotel, tel. 631134
San Carlo, tel. 630697
Bassacutena, tel. 659621

Tharros

Situated on the promontory of Capo San Marco which reaches out
into the sea to form a natural double harbour typical of the
Phoenician colonies, the old Carthaginian-Roman town of Tharros
retains traces of its ancient splendour. Abandoned around the year
1000 following Saracen raids, Tharros was rediscovered in the
1950s, and its network of streets is still well preserved, along with a
perfect sewage system, numerous remains of dwellings and
religious buildings, including a very fine monolithic Carthaginian
temple, and civic buildings including two thermal establishments.
Traces of an early Christian baptistry indicate that the town was
inhabited at least as late as the 5th century AD. The church of San
Giovanni, built around the 10th century on a domed base dating
from the 6th century, has a simple interior with three naves, barrel
vaults and a baptismal font bearing the early Christian symbol of
the fish.

Nearby
Nearby is the village of San Salvatore, containing a little church
standing on the site of the underground tomb of the same name,
dating from the 4th century AD. Going down a long staircase you
will find four chambers with interesting figure drawings. The tomb
was probably linked with the pagan cult of the waters, and later
used as a place for Christian worship, while in medieval times it
was even used as a prison.

Villacidro

This little town on the slopes of Monte Linas is surrounded by the green of olive and citrus groves, while a road leads directly from the town to the lovely waterfall 'Sa Spendula', which plunges over a precipice in an attractive setting of rocks, pine trees and oaks.

USEFUL ADDRESSES

TOURIST INFORMATION
Piazza Incani, tel. 791393

HOTEL
E.S.I.T. Sa Spendula, tel. 9329233

TRAVEL AGENCY
Sa Spendula, Via Regione Sarda, tel. 932240

Villanovaforru

Just outside the village of Villanovaforru, at the point known as 'Genna Maria,' are the spectacular archaeological excavations that recently brought to light one of the most interesting Nuraghic settlements in Sardinia and made famous the name of this little village that was almost unknown until a short time ago.

Around an original tower, the excavations have uncovered a whole series of smaller, secondary buildings that once served civil and 'industrial' purposes, producing a large part of the Nuraghic pottery used in the area. These items, and other articles found that bear witness to the level of civilisation attained by the inhabitants of the ancient settlement, are now exhibited in a functional museum in the centre of the village. The visitor is struck by the modern design of the pottery pieces, which have shapes and dimensions of an almost futuristic beauty. The museum also houses articles from the Carthaginian-Roman period found in the village and in the surrounding area.

Villasimius

A pleasant resort area, this is one of the main new holiday settlements on the south-east corner of Sardinia which, with the new developments at Costa Rei, stretch almost all the way to Muravera.

USEFUL ADDRESSES

TOURIST INFORMATION
Piazza Incani, tel. 791393

HOTELS
Altura, tel. 791168
Il Bolognese, tel. 791272
Simius Playa, tel. 791227

Zuri

Before flooding the valley to create the Lake Omodeo, a precious jewel of Romanesque architecture was dismantled stone by stone and rebuilt here at Zuri: the church of San Pietro. This fine monument in coral pink trachyte, built towards the end of the 13th century, is made particularly imposing by its original bell-tower. Nearby is the gigantic Nuraghe Losa, one of the most important traces of the civilisation that developed in Sardinia between the 15th and 16th century BC. Around the original three-storey conical tower, perhaps used as a place of worship, stand the fortified walls that made the complex a defensive stronghold.

USEFUL INFORMATION

'The heaviest baggage for a traveller is an empty purse.'

GERMAN PROVERB

WHEN TO GO TO SARDINIA

Sardinia's climate is mild all the year round, but the best period for a visit is between May and October, when many of the island's most colourful festivals take place. In July and August the coastal resorts become very crowded with holidaymaking Italians and, like those of neighbouring Corsica, tend to close almost completely from autumn to spring. The island lies in the path of some powerful winds, and these can blow, non-stop, for several days, so it is useful to take some warmer clothing with you, especially if you plan to stay in, or visit, the mountainous regions.

AVERAGE TEMPERATURES °C
Cagliari

Jan	Feb	Mar	Apr	May	Jun	Jul	Aug	Sep	Oct	Nov	Dec
9.9	10.3	12.9	15.3	18.6	22.8	25.8	25.7	23.3	19.5	15.6	11.8

Average temperatures in mountain locations taken over the last 25 years: spring 11.6, summer 21.8, autumn, 15.3, winter 6.2
Water temperatures: April 14.5, May 16.5, June 20.0, July 23.0, august 24.0; September 23.0; October 21.0.

HOW TO GET TO SARDINIA

BY AIR
As is the case with Corsica, there are no direct, non-stop scheduled flights to Sardinia from the UK. Instead, both Alitalia and British Airways operate frequent one-stop year-round scheduled services, the most popular routings being via Rome or Milan to the

Sardinian airports of Alghero, Cagliari or Olbia. Alitalia, for
instance, operates from London (Heathrow) to Rome twice a day
and to Milan three times a day. From Rome there are twice-daily
non-stop services to Alghero and seven flights a day to Cagliari;
and from Milan three flights a day to Alghero. The only internal
flights are between Alghero and Cagliari on ATI lines, and
between Cagliari and Olbia on Alisarda Airlines.

The Rome to Alghero flights take about 55 minutes, to Cagliari
55 minutes and to Olbia 45 minutes; while the journey from Milan
to Alghero takes about 70 minutes, to Cagliari 80 minutes and to
Olbia 65 minutes. There are also flights to Cagliari from Bologna,
and to Olbia from Brindisi.

In addition to the scheduled services routed by the Italian
mainland, there are frequent direct charter flights from Britain in
the summer months to Sardinia's three airports: Cagliari-Elmas,
Alghero and Sassari-Fertilia, and Olbia. Travel agents should be
able to supply you with the relevant brochures and information.

BY SEA
Car/passenger ferries operate to Sardinia from Livorno, Genoa
and Civitavecchia. The Civitavecchia-Olbia run is the shortest,
taking between seven and eight hours. Space is booked way ahead,
and it is always advisable to reserve your return passage at the
same time; there are also frequent ferry services by Tirrenia and
others to the offshore islets of Carloforte and La Maddelena.

There are several daily connections throughout the year,
increasing substantially in the summer; nearly all are overnight
services.

Grand Traghetti, which operates shipping services from mainland
Italy to Sardinia, is represented in the UK by Associated Oceanic
Agencies, Eagle House, 109–110 Jermyn Street, London SW1,
tel. 01–930 5683

Tirrenia Lines, which also operates Italy to Sardinia (and Italy to
Corsica services), can be contacted c/o Serena Holidays, 40–42
Kenway Road, London SW5, tel. 01–373 6548.

Société Nationale Maritime Corse-Mediterranee, c/o Continental
Shipping and Travel, 179 Piccadilly, London W1, tel. 01–491 4968,
operates from France to Sardinia.

Tirrenia Lines and other companies operate local services, for example La Maddalena – Santa Teresa di Gallura – Bonifacio (Corsica); Santa Teresa di Gallura – La Maddalena; Carloforte – Portovesme; La Maddalena – Bonifacio; La Maddalena – Palau, etc.

Grandi Traghetti Lines operates frequent services to Porto Torres from Genoa.

Italian Railways operate several daily crossings from Civitavecchia to Golfo Aranci, with a service increased during the summer months. For passengers travelling by car bookings are obligatory from 16 July to 12 August from Civitavecchia, and from 16 August to 12 September from Golfo Aranci to Civitavecchia.

BY ROAD

Tourists who take their car to Italy are entitled to a reduction on the normal price of petrol (supergrade only) and the motorway tolls. This concession applies to all cars with a foreign registration number, but it excludes commercial vehicles. The petrol coupons cannot be paid for in Italian currency and are not available for purchase in Italy itself. A specific package exists for tourists visiting southern Italy, which includes all regions south of Rome (excluding Rome itself): southern Latium, Abruzzi, Molise, Campania, Apulia, Bastilicata, Calabria, Sicily and Sardinia. This package includes coupons for 150 litres of petrol plus an extra 200-litre voucher to be used in southern Italy and 13 motorway vouchers. These 200-litre vouchers can be exchanged for petrol coupons once in Sardinia or elsewhere in southern Italy at the Italian Automobile Club Offices (ACI). Petrol coupons and motorway vouchers are issued along with a Fuel Card (Carta Carburante) which is necessary to take advantage of the free breakdown service provided by ACI to foreign motorists.

The Italian State Tourist Office has appointed C.I.T. (50 Conduit Street, London W1. tel. 01–434 3844) agents for the sale of these petrol coupons.

The same packages are also available from the A.A. and R.A.C. and at the Italian frontier points from the Italian Automobile Club offices. Passport and car log-book are necessary for their purchase, and they are available only to personal callers on production of these documents. They will not be issued on behalf of other people.

CAR HIRE

Those not wishing to take their own car to Sardinia will have no problem hiring one when they arrive, since most of the major international car rental companies are widely represented, with offices not only at the airports and principal points of entry, but also in the major tourist resorts. In addition, a huge number of local firms offer car hire, with rates that are sometimes cheaper than the big-name companies.

Rates generally include breakdown service, maintenance, oil, seat belts, but not petrol. Basic insurance is also included but additional cover is available at fixed rates. Most firms require a deposit equal to the estimated cost of hire, and VAT at 18% will be added to the total cost. Some car rental companies restrict hire to drivers over 21 years of age, but generally you must have had a valid driving licence for at last one year before applying for car-hire.

Motor scooters are also widely available for hire.

GREEN CARD INSURANCE

It is advisable to take out Green Card insurance if you intend taking your car to Sardinia or hiring one there. A British driving licence is valid, but must be accompanied by a translation which is obtainable from C.I.T., A.C.I., frontier and provincial Offices, and also the Italian State Tourist Office in London, free of charge.

BY RAIL

Tickets from London and from British ports to many Italian towns are printed and issued by British Rail and their agents with a validity of two months; additional journeys or circular tours can be arranged in advance through a travel agency with a validity of two months. The journeys can be begun on any day within the period of validity, calculated from midnight to midnight and inclusive of the date of commencement, and break of journey is allowed at any number of intermediate stations en route without formality, for tickets purchased in Great Britain.

Italian Railways operates several daily crossings from Civitavecchia, near Rome, to the Sardinian holiday resort and port of Golfo degli Aranci. The service is increased during the peak summer months, when car bookings are obligatory.

Children: on Italian and British railways children under the age of four (not occupying a seat) travel free. Between the ages of four and twelve a reduction of 50% is granted, while the same reduction is also granted by French, Belgian and Luxembourg Railways for children between the ages of four and twelve (on Swiss Railways between the ages of six and 16).

Inter-Rail and Senior Citizen Cards: for young people up to 26 years of age a card is available from British Rail and its appointed agents giving a reduction of 50% for travel by British Rail and free travel on the national railways of some 20 European countries, including Italy. Senior citizens (men over 65, women over 60), can buy a yearly card which provides 30% reductions. Details of validity and travel restrictions can be obtained from Italian State Railways, C.I.T., or from branches of Thomas Cook.

Ferrovie dello Stato serves the Cagliari-Oristano-Macomer-Sassari-Porto Torres line, with a branch off at Chilivari for Olbia and Golfo Aranci. There are usually several trains a day on weekdays. The trip running the length of the island takes about five hours. In addition there are several subsidiary lines: one from Bosa to Nuoro, intersecting the main line at Macomer, and one to Carbonia-Iglesias-Decimomannu-Cagliari. Two old narrow-guage lines are still in service: a scenic trip through the Barbagia from Cagliari to Mandas-Sevi-Lanusei-Arbatax, and the Alghero-Sassari-Tempio Pausania-Palau route operated by the Strade Ferrate Sarde (SFS).

TRAVELLING AROUND

Like Sicily, and unlike Corsica, getting around Sardinia is relatively easy. Rail and bus systems are cheap, comparatively efficient and extensive. Unfortunately, most of Sardinia's attractions, natural wonders and Pisan churches, are out in the country, and if you intend to see more than a few of them, you will need a car.

It is possible to reach nearly every village from its provincial capital but sometimes tricky, since buses are understandably arranged for the convenience of the villagers as opposed to tourists, meaning that schedules can be a problem. If you are making a day trip out to a village, check in advance if there is a bus coming back when you need it.

BUS
As almost everywhere in Italy, riding the bus in Sardinia is almost a pleasure. The lines are subsidised by the state, so the fares are

cheap, and the coaches themselves are usually new and clean. From each of the four provincial Sardinian capitals regular services run to all the towns and villages in the province. In Cagliari and Oristano, the company is SATAS; in Nuoro and Sassari it is ARST. Services between the provincial capitals are provided by the PANI line.

PASSPORTS AND VISAS

British subjects require either a passport or a visitor's card to enter Sardinia.

POLICE REGISTRATION
Police registration is required within three days of entering mainland Italy or its islands, including Sardinia. If staying at an hotel the management will attend to the formality, but the visitor is responsible for checking that this has been carried out. Your permit to stay in Sardinia will last three months as a tourist; should you wish to stay for a longer period, an extension must be obtained from the Police.

ACCOMMODATION

Sardinia has a good selection of hotels, many of them new or comparatively modern, and at least in the popular holiday areas standards tend to be as high as, if not higher than, those on neighbouring Corsica. Hotels are classified into five categories: deluxe, first, second, third, fourth; pensions into three categories: first, second, third. Every hotel and pension has its fixed charges agreed with the provincial tourist board and these vary according to class, season, services available and locality. In all hotels and pensions service charges are included in the rates, while VAT (TVA in Italy) operates in all hotels at 10% (18% deluxe hotels) on room charges only. As far as rates are concerned, first class pensions correspond usually to second class hotels; second class pensions to third class hotels; and third class pensions to fourth class hotels. Visitors are now required by law to obtain an official receipt when staying at hotels.

HOTEL LISTS
Hotel lists and resort leaflets are produced by provincial tourist boards (Ente Provinciale per il Turismo) and by the local tourist offices (Azienda Autonoma di Soggiorno) of the various cities and resorts in Sardinia. They can be obtained by writing direct to the office of the town concerned.

COTTAGES AND FARMHOUSES
The renting of holiday cottages or farmhouses in Sardinia is becoming increasingly popular. Numerous travel companies specialise in this field, but further information can be obtained from Agriturist Comitato Regionale, c/o Federazione Agricoltori, V. le Trieste 6, 09100 Cagliari, tel. 070-668330

STUDENT HOSTEL
The student hostel in Sassari is available not only to students taking courses but also to students visiting the island for holiday purposes. Applications should be made to 'Casa dello Studente,' Sassari.

VILLAS, FLATS AND CHALETS
Villas, flats and chalets are available to rent at most Sardinian resorts. Information can be obtained through the tourist office (Azienda Autonoma di Soggiorno) of the locality concerned, through daily newspapers or through specialised travel companies.

EATING AND DRINKING

Sardinian food is quite distinctive, and on the whole, tasty and of good quality, although perhaps lacking the variety of mainland cooking. Famous among the island's great variety of local breads is carta da musica (literally, music paper), baked of semola flour in wafer-thin round sheets until it is very crisp. It is very tasty and keeps for weeks at a time: in fact, it is the daily bread of the shepherds who live in the rugged hills with their flocks and only occasionally return to their villages for provisions. Bread, indeed, is as much an art form as a staple, and some special kinds are baked for special occasions: in the shape of towers, or castles for weddings, or something that looks almost like lace.

Antipasti may be seafood salads or plates of sausages (salsiccia) and local prosciutto, sometimes of cinghiale (boar). Bottarga (fish roe) appears on menus as an antipasto or as a condiment for pasta.

Most restaurant menus on Sardinia will feature some variety of Sardinian pasta, the most typical being *malloreddus*, sometimes called *gnocchetti sardi*, usually served with sausage sauce and plenty of the island's famous *pecorino*, sheep's-milk cheese.

Culurrones is the island version of ravioli, while there are many kinds of minestra (vegetable soups with or without pasta). *Zuppa cuata* is a delicious, dense, oven-baked soup that combines layers of bread, cheese, tomato sauce, all moistened with broth, and *zu ziminu* is fish soup.

Porceddu (roast suckling pig) and spit-roasted lamb or kid appear on some regional menus – though they are becoming increasingly difficult to find – and occasionally more exotic traditional dishes, in which thrushes and blackbirds and the entrails of various animals figure prominently, such as *accarraxiau* or *sa frixioredda*. Sardinia is also famous for wonderful artichokes, and a few kinds of strong cheese.

Coastal areas are best for fish: *aragosta* (lobster) is a speciality but is it usually expensive – as, indeed, it is on Corsica. An exquisite dessert, sebadas, or seadas, is a light, cheese-filled ravioli that is fried and covered with wild honey. Suspirus is an almond confection.

Wine is, on the whole, excellent and cheap – much better than in Corsica. The island is best known for desert wines of a formidable alcoholic content, such as the *Vernaccia* of Oristano and Sulcis, which is dry and golden and relatively high in alcoholic content. Every province has its wine making regions, and some of the best wine, such as *Anghelu Ruiu* (red) and *Torbato* (white) comes from Alghero. Other varieties include *Muscatel, Aleatico* and the strong *Cannonau.*

Many restaurants in Sardinia offer a special tourist menu (Menu turistico) at an all-inclusive fixed price. Bars are open from early morning until late at night and can serve any kind of snacks, refreshments, drinks etc. When a drink is served at your table an extra charge is made.

Vegetarians can obtain advice on where to eat from the Associazione Vegetariana Italiana, Viale Gran Sasso 38, Milan, or from the London Vegetarian Society, 53 Marloes Road, London W8.

SHOPPING

Shops are generally open from 08.30 or 09.00 to 13.00 and again from 15.30 or 16.00 to 19.30 or 20.00, though in some of the resorts the lunch break is shorter and shops close earlier. Supermarkets can be found in the main towns and resorts, while baby food can be bought anywhere at chemists (farmacia), supermarkets and grocers.

BANKING HOURS

Banks are usually open in the morning from 08.30 to 13.30 and one hour in the afternoon, from 15.00 to 16.00, but it is advisable to check locally as times of opening in the afternoon vary from bank to bank. They are not open on Saturdays and Sundays and other national holidays. Travellers' cheques and bank cheques can be exchanged at most hotels, and visitors can also change foreign money at main railway stations and airports.

FISHING
The waters surrounding Sardinia are ideal for underwater fishing, although it should be noted that underwater fishing with aqualungs in all Italian waters is not permitted, though their use is allowed for other purposes. Sea sport fishing may be practised both from the shore and from a boat, but a special permit issued by the Harbourmaster's Office is sometimes required.

Only those over the age of 16 are allowed to use underwater guns and such equipment. When submerged, an underwater fisherman is required to indicate the fact with a float bearing a red flag with a yellow diagonal stripe, and must operate within a radius of 50 m of the support barge or the float bearing the flag. Fishing is prohibited at under 500 m from a beach used by bathers, and 50 m from fishing installations and ships at anchor.

FRESHWATER FISHING
For fishing in rivers, streams, lakes and in all inland public and free freshwaters, a Government licence issued by the provincial administration is required. A licence for rod-fishing with or without a reel is valid for one year. With the exception of about ten per cent, which are reserved for private use, all the remaining waters liable to exclusive fishing rights are managed by the Italian Angling Federation. Fishing in private waters requires the owner's permission, while fishing in all other waters requires the Federation membership card, which can be obtained without

special formalities at all provincial sections, federate associations, or the head office, Viale Tiziano, 70 Roma.

F.I.P.S. membership for foreigners is valid for one year and allows fishing in all waters of the federations listed in a special brochure which is issued together with the card, giving information on fishing conditions, minimum fish sizes, non-fishing periods and other useful regulations.

Fishing in all inland waters is generally satisfactory. Mountain waters, or at least those situated at over 600 m above sea-level, normally contain salmonids (trout, grayling, char); the other waters contain various species, mainly bleak, chub, carp, tench, pike, perch, roach, etc. In most towns and even villages in Sardinia suitable bait and fishing equipment for local requirements can be bought.

The organisation in charge of both salt-water and fresh water fishing in Italy is the Italian Sport Fishing Federation (Federazione Italiana della Pesca Sportiva). Every provincial capital has a section where the foreign tourist, in addition to the federation membership card, can get all the necessary instructions to fish to the best advantage in the area concerned, and information on fish-size restrictions and limits on fishing times and places as laid down by the laws and regulations both for freshwater and salt-water fishing.

YACHTING
The Sardinian coastline, with its many natural harbours and delightful new man-made marinas, is ideal for yachting. As a rule permission to anchor should be obtained from the Capitaneri di Porto (Harbour Master). In ports where special berths are allotted to yachts, members of recognised yacht clubs may use them.

REGULATIONS
● No customs papers are needed for boats with or without engines or when brought by car and having the same number plate. Under International Customs Regulations they can normally remain in Italy for six months.
● Boats brought by car do not require insurance, but must be inspected by a Port Authority before entering the water.
● The captain of a boat arriving by sea must report to the Port Authority with boat papers and crew passports.
● At the first Port a document called a 'Costituto' will be issued, which must be shown at subsequent ports of call, and which also

enables fuel to be bought exempt from tax. The 'Costituto' must be surrendered when leaving Italian water.

- Boats with engines exceeding 3 hp require insurance
- Boats with engines must carry a number plate
- Boats remaining in Italy for a long temporary period must carry a Navigation Licence from their country of origin. Visitors leaving a boat in Italy are exempt from taxes for one year.
- A tax must be paid by all yachts (Italian or foreign) when berthed at any Italian port, including those in Sardinia. The levy is reduced by two-thirds in the case of a two-month subscription between June and September, by half when the subscription is for the entire June-September period, and by half for a 12 month subscription.

Driving licences are not required for the following:–

Length not exceeding 5 m, engine not above 120 hp and sails not more than 14 sq m.

Sailing boats (with auxiliary engine) for sailing within 20 miles from the coast.

Boats with engines not exceeding 3 BRT inboard or outboard, and not above 20 hp for nagivation within 20 miles from coast.

Foreigners carrying an Ability Document from their country of origin may sail the craft for which they are qualified.

INDEX

CORSICA

References in italics indicate a major entry on the subject

INDEX

SARDINIA

References in italics indicate a major entry on the subject